New England

HOUSE
MUSEUMS

A Guide to More than 100 Mansions,
Cottages, and Historical Sites

ROBERT J. REGALBUTO

THE COUNTRYMAN PRESS
A division of W. W. Norton & Company
Independent Publishers Since 1923

Manufacturing by Versa Press
Book design by Chris Welch
Production manager: Devon Zahn

The Countryman Press
www.countrymanpress.com

A division of W. W. Norton & Company, Inc.,
500 Fifth Avenue, New York, NY 10110
www.wwnorton.com

978-1-58157-497-5 (pbk.)

10 9 8 7 6 5 4 3 2 1

New England

HOUSE
MUSEUMS

Contents

MASSACHUSETTS

NEW HAMPSHIRE

RHODE ISLAND

VERMONT

Acknowledgments

"Gratitude is not only the greatest of virtues,
but the parent of all others."
—MARCUS TULLIUS CICERO

My sincere thanks go to those who have helped make this book possible: David Boenning, Martha and Peter Borovec, Dwight Cook, Patrick Coran, Mary Finn Cox, John Hinman, Donald Kantor, Coleman Kelly, Helder Lemos, Derick Martins, Jay McDaniel, Joyce Novak, Bruce Peters, and Dennis Walker.

A particular word of thanks to my brother, Joseph F. P. Regalbuto Jr., for his many hours reviewing the manuscript and for offering valued commentary.

Introduction

"The lines are fallen unto [us] in pleasant places;
yea, [we] have a goodly heritage."

—PSALM 16

House museums are windows on the past. They are tangible links to America's history and allow us to walk where our predecessors walked, to see the objects they touched, the books they read, and the interiors, gardens, and landscapes they saw.

More than one hundred historic houses are described in this guide. All are within the six states that make up New England. They date from the early seventeenth century to the threshold of our time, and the architectural styles reflect those which were popular over a period of four centuries. The homes of leaders and literati, merchants and millionaires, poets and Pilgrims, philosophers and farmers, seafarers and Shakers: These sites are crucial pieces of American history.

Each chapter lists the museum's location, web address, and telephone number. As operating schedules often change from season to season and from year to year, and as admission fees can be ephemeral, they are not included here. Readers are encouraged to contact the house museum in advance of their visit for up-to-date visiting information.

It is my sincere hope that this guide will lead you, the reader, to townhouses, homesteads, mansions, farms, and castles which will be your windows on New England's past and our "goodly heritage."

CONNECTICUT

GILLETTE CASTLE

Michael King / iStockphoto
.com

Gillette Castle

67 River Road
East Haddam, CT 06423
Phone: 860-526-2336
www.ct.gov.deep/gillettecastle

Sited on the last and most southerly of the chain of hills known as the Seven Sisters, this estate was first named, appropriately, the Seventh Sister. The castle is the creation of William Hook Gillette (1853–1937), an actor, playwright, director, and novelist. Gillette designed every detail of his castle, including its gardens. It took a crew of twenty men five years to build his dream castle, which was completed in 1919. Differing from medieval European prototypes, Gillette's castle has a steel frame and is faced with local fieldstones. The Craftsman-style interior has hand-hewn southern white oak throughout.

Gillette spared no details. He fitted his home with personally designed features like built-in sofas, a table on tracks, forty-seven uniquely designed doors, door knobs, and locks. A series of hidden mirrors allowed him to keep an eye on the castle's rooms (and guests!) from the vantage point of his bedroom.

Gillette's creativity extended to the grounds of his 142-acre estate. He had a narrow-gauge railroad with its own "Grand Central Station," a wooden trestle bridge, a tunnel, walking paths, and a goldfish pond. The railroad tracks have since been pulled up and replaced with an additional walking trail.

William Hook Gillette died in 1937. In his will, he expressed his wish that his beloved estate not fall victim to a "blithering sap-head who has no conception of where he is or with what surrounded." He would be pleased to know that Gillette Castle became the property of the state of Connecticut in 1943. The house went through an $11 million dollar restoration that was completed in 2002.

Hill-Stead Museum

35 Mountain Road
Farmington, CT 06032
Phone: 860-677-4787
www.hillstead.org

"A great new house on a hillside."

—HENRY JAMES

Hill-Stead Museum was the creation of Theodate Pope Riddle (1867–1946). She grew up in Cleveland and first came to Farmington to attend Miss Porter's School. She survived the sinking of the *Lusitania* when it was torpedoed in 1915 and married Wallace Riddle the following year.

Mrs. Riddle was one of America's first women to be trained as an architect, and Hill-Stead was her first building design. She worked with the firm of McKim, Mead, & White in drawing up the plans. The house was built for her father, Alfred Atmore Pope, between 1898 and 1901, and Theodate later inherited it from her parents. When she died in 1946, she willed that it be a memorial to them and a museum "for the benefit and enjoyment of the public." She further stipulated that it remain as she left it, with its original furnishings and artwork.

A white Colonial Revival house porch, with its tall columns, is somewhat reminiscent of that at George Washington's home, Mount Vernon. The interior has nineteen gracious rooms covering 33,000 square feet. Both Theodate and her parents were collectors of art, especially Impressionist works. There are paintings by Claude Monet, Mary Cassatt, Édouard Manet, Edgar Degas, James McNeill Whistler, and others.

The 152-acre estate includes an eighteenth-century farm house, a barn, farm buildings, a carriage house with a theater, broad lawns, a newly restored sunken garden, an octagonal flower garden, and a pond.

The Mark Twain House and Museum

351 Farmington Avenue
Hartford, CT 06105
Phone: 860-247-0998
www.marktwainhouse.org

"It is a home—and the word never had so much meaning before."

—MARK TWAIN

Mark Twain, the "greatest American humorist of his age" and the "father of American literature," first came to Hartford in 1868. At that time the city was a major publishing center. He and his wife, Olivia (Livy), moved to Hartford in 1871, and their newly built home was completed in 1874. Some of his best-loved works were written here, including *A Connecticut Yankee in King Arthur's Court, The Adventures of Tom Sawyer, The Adventures of Huckleberry Finn, The Prince and the Pauper, The Gilded Age,* and *Life on the Mississippi.*

Architect Edward Tuckerman Potter designed the house in the Victorian Gothic style. The house was renovated and enlarged in 1881. In the end, Twain's costs were $31,000 for the land, $70,000 for the house, and $22,000 for its furnishings.

Though Twain was a successful author, he lost a good portion of his earnings through poor investments. For additional income, he decided to lecture in Europe in 1895 and 1896, traveling with Livy and their daughter Clara. Their other daughters, Jean and Susy, remained at home in Hartford. Susy died of spinal meningitis while her parents were in Europe. Following this, Mark and Livy sold their Hartford house in 1903.

The house was subsequently used as a school, a library, and an apartment house. It was saved from the wrecker's ball in 1929 and restored between 1955 and 1974. A major, multi-million–dollar renovation was completed in 1999, and in 2003 the Webster Bank Museum Center was opened.

Today, the Mark Twain House has the only intact Louis Comfort Tiffany & Co. interior in existence. This twenty-five-room house maintains a collection of some fifty thousand objects: furnishings, fixtures, Tiffany

glass, artwork, memorabilia, and manuscripts. The Museum Center has a permanent exhibit on the author's life, and special exhibits are mounted. A documentary on Twain's life produced by Ken Burns is shown in the theatre, and the house also features a store, a café, and a patio.

THE MARK TWAIN
HOUSE

SeanPavonePhoto /
iStockphoto.com

Harriet Beecher Stowe Center

77 Forest Avenue

Hartford, CT 06105

Phone: 860-522-9258

www.harrietbeecherstowecenter.org

"The little woman who wrote the book that made this great war."

—ABRAHAM LINCOLN

"Next door to Twain I found Mrs. Harriet Beecher Stowe, a
wonderfully agile old lady, as fresh as a squirrel still, but with the
face and air of a lion."

—HENRY DRUMMOND

Harriet Beecher Stowe (1811–1896) was a significant figure in the abolitionist movement in antebellum America. She and her husband, Calvin Ellis Stowe (1802–1886), supported and participated in the Underground Railroad, providing temporary shelter to fugitive slaves en route to Canada. She was also a prolific author, having penned works as varied as novels, biographies, children's textbooks, and books on home economics, child rearing, and religious subjects. But she is best remembered for *Uncle Tom's Cabin*. First a novel and later a play and a film, this 1852 work portrayed the lives of American slaves. It was a bestseller in its time and greatly advanced the cause of abolition.

This house was built in 1871 for the Chamberlin family and sold to the Stowes in 1873. It is a Gothic Revival "cottage orne," and its exterior paint colors were chosen by Harriet in 1878. The house has fourteen rooms and is 4,500 square feet. After she died here in 1896, the house had several owners. In 1924, a descendant, Katherine Seymour Day, bought the house and lived in it for forty years. She gathered family memorabilia and objects which had belonged to Stowe—furniture, decorative items, pictures, family photos, books, and manuscripts—and brought them here with the intent of making this house a museum one day. The collection also includes paintings done by Harriet Beecher Stowe herself. The dining room, kitchen, parlor, and bedrooms are all part of the house tour.

The Glass House

199 Elm Street
New Canaan, CT 06840
Phone: 203-594-9884
http://theglasshouse.org

> *"All architecture is shelter, all great architecture is the design of space*
> *that contains, cuddles, exalts, or stimulates the persons in that space."*
>
> —PHILIP JOHNSON

The Glass House was designed by, and built for, outstanding American post-modernist architect Philip Johnson (1906–2005), and it served as the owner's weekend home for nearly sixty years. Inspired by 1920s German architects and more directly by Mies van der Rohe's Farnsworth House in Illinois, Johnson built the Glass House in 1949. Strikingly modern and innovative, it is a flat-roofed, rectangular building, its four glass walls enclosing an open space with low walnut cabinets dividing a dining room, kitchen, and sleeping area. Only a brick cylinder, enclosing the bath, breaks the space from floor to ceiling. Some of the furniture was designed by van der Rohe.

But there is a lot more to this property than the Glass House. This large estate originally had forty-seven acres. There are thirteen buildings on the property designed by Johnson, spanning the years from 1949 to 1995. The Brick House, built in 1949, served as the guest house. In later years Johnson moved to the Brick House and used the Glass House only for entertaining. Some of the other buildings here include the Painting Gallery, the Sculpture Gallery, the Study, the Pavilion, the Ghost House, and Kirstein Tower. The last construction project was Da Monsta, the entrance gate.

THE GLASS HOUSE

fdastudillo / iStockphoto.com

Florence Griswold Museum

96 Lyme Street
Old Lyme, CT 06371
Phone: 860-434-5542
http://florencegriswoldmuseum.org

> *"I saw a charming house that appeared like a Roman temple among*
> *the trees. Admiringly, I beheld the broad steps surmounted by*
> *four huge ionic columns that towered to the roof and formed a*
> *magnificent adornment to the mansion's front, the handsome old*
> *doorway of which stood hospitably open."*
>
> —ARTHUR HEMING

At the end of the nineteenth century and at the beginning of the twentieth, Old Lyme was America's best-known art colony. It was a center for the budding Impressionist movement in America.

Florence Griswold (1850–1937) opened her home as a boarding house for artists. That hospitality was extended to President Woodrow Wilson and his family when they dined here with Miss Griswold and her artist boarders.

The house dates to 1817, and its interior appears as it did in 1910. On the first floor, the central hall is a gallery hung with paintings by some of the artists who lived here. This leads to the parlor, where the artists would gather and entertain, the dining room, the bedroom used by "Miss Florence," and a guest room. Probably the most enchanting and unique features of the house are the artists' paintings, forty-one in all, painted on wall panels and door panels. On the second floor there are exhibit galleries.

Just steps away from the house is the Kreble Gallery. Completed in 2001, it has a permanent collection of works by John F. Kensett, Frederic Church, Childe Hassam, and others. The property also has the studio of artist William Chadwick (1879–1962) and gardens and grounds.

THE DINING ROOM,
FLORENCE GRISWOLD
MUSEUM

*Joe Standart photo courtesy of
Florence Griswold Museum*

Houses of the Webb-Deane-Stevens Museum

211 Main Street
Old Wethersfield, CT 06109
Phone: 860-529-0612
http://webb-deane-stevens.org

The neighborhood known today as Old Wethersfield was founded in 1634 by ten Puritan men and is Connecticut's largest historic district. Within its two square miles there are 1,100 buildings which date to the seventeenth, eighteenth, and nineteenth centuries.

Buttolph-Williams House

The Buttolph-Williams house was built in 1714 for Benjamin Belden and his wife, Anne Churchill. It came into the hands of the Antiquarian and Landmarks Society in 1941, and it was restored and then opened to the public as a museum in 1951.

This is a two-and-a-half-story timber-frame house with a one-and-a-half-story addition, an unadorned front door, a steeply pitched roof, and a large central chimney. It has much of its original wood: the timber framing, floorboards, doors, and interior woodwork. Much of the stonework is original as well: the fireplaces, chimney, and foundation. The house has an outstanding collection of late-seventeenth-century furniture and household objects.

Isaac Stevens House

This house was completed in 1789, and here Isaac Stevens, a leatherworker, not only lived but also worked. The kitchen doubled as a work area for Mr. and Mrs. Stevens.

The first floor of this house is furnished as it might have been in the 1820s and 1830s. The furniture and decorative items are true to the period and the wallpapers are accurate reproductions of the originals.

The rooms and exhibits on the second floor tell us much about the life of nineteenth-century children. The childrens' bedroom is furnished for five children, and the paint colors are the originals as discovered during the course of restoration in the 1960s. Other rooms display the Colonial Dames collection of dolls, dollhouses, and other toys.

Joseph Webb House

This Georgian-style house was built in 1752 for merchant Joseph Webb IV (c. 1727–1761). He and his wife, Mehitabel Nott (c.1732–1767), had six children. Joseph died at the age of thirty-four. The executor of his will, Silas Deane, married the widow Mehitabel and built the home just next door. The Webb house then passed to son Joseph Webb Jr. The younger Joseph and his wife made this house a center for lavish parties and gatherings, and they accommodated overnight guests. It became known as "Hospitality Hall," and justifiably so. General George Washington (1732–1799) was here for five days and five nights in 1781. Here he met with the French General comte de Rochambeau (1725–1807) to strategize in planning the Battle of Yorktown.

Webb sold the house in 1790. It had various owners before it was bought by Judge Martin Welles (1787–1863) in 1820. It remained in the Welles family until it transferred to Wallace Nutting (1861–1941) in 1913. Nutting was a well known champion of the Colonial Revival movement. He was a photographer, and his subjects were New England landscapes, colonial buildings, and early American furniture. An astute businessman, Nutting sold his photographs. He also manufactured and sold reproductions of colonial-period furniture. Mr. Nutting commissioned a series of murals depicting scenes from colonial times for the hall and parlors in the Joseph Webb House. He did this to add appeal to the house as one stop on his "Chain of Colonial Picture Houses." Tours were given here, and there was a shop in which his photographs, books, and furniture were sold. With the advent of World War I and gasoline rations, fewer folks were able to travel. The Joseph Webb House failed as a Nutting business venture, and in 1919 he sold the property to the National Society of the Colonial Dames of America, which restored the property and maintains this house museum. There is a special exhibit here dedicated to Wallace Nutting, his work, and his legacy.

Silas Deane House

Mehitabel Nott Webb, widow of the elder Joseph Webb, married her attorney and business advisor Silas Deane (1737–1789). In 1766 they built this house just steps from Mehitabel's former home. Mehitabel died the following year, leaving Silas with their son and her six children from her previous marriage. Deane then married another wealthy widow, Elizabeth Saltonstall Evards, in 1769.

Silas was a Yale College graduate. In 1774, he was a delegate to the Second Continental Congress. Known as America's first foreign diplomat, he became the country's envoy to France in 1778. There he lodged with Benjamin Franklin, and they helped to secure a treaty of alliance with France. Deane died in England in 1790.

Over the course of the next century or more, there was a series of owners. The last was Mrs. Margaret Clark Fenn. A Colonial Dame, she willed the house to The National Society of Colonial Dames of America in Connecticut. The Dames meticulously restored the house from 1960 to 1974.

On entering this two-story house, visitors are treated to an impressively large and light-filled hall. The carved balustrades on the grand staircase are original, as is much of the other woodwork. One of the mantels is made from brownstone from Portland, Connecticut. Portraits of the Deanes greet visitors when they enter the parlor.

Roseland Cottage

556 Route 169
Woodstock, CT 06281
Phone: 860-928-4074
www.historicnewengland.org/historicproperties/homes/
roseland-cottage/roseland-cottage

Roseland Cottage overlooks the picturesque town common in the Woodstock Hill Historic District. It was built in 1846 for Woodstock native Henry C. Bowen (1813–1896). When he was twenty years old, Bowen went to New York City to seek his fortune and found it there as a merchant of silks and other fine fabrics. There he met his wife, Lucy Maria Tappan (1825–1863), whose family had also made its fortune in the dry goods business. They had ten children. Seeking refuge from hot city summers, Bowen returned to Woodstock to build this, a summer home for his family. By the 1870s, the Bowens were hosting large Independence Day celebrations at Roseland Cottage, in time attended by four US presidents. The last Bowen descendant to live here was Henry's granddaughter Constance, who died in 1968 at the age of eighty-nine. Two years later the property, the house, and its contents were bought by the Society for the Preservation of New England Antiquities (SPNEA), today known as Historic New England, which opened them to the public as a museum.

English architect Joseph C. Wells (1814–1860) designed the home in the Carpenter Gothic (or Gothic Revival) style, drawing inspiration from medieval sources. This "cottage orne," or decorative cottage, is distinguished by its steeply gabled roofs and dormers, "gingerbread" ornamenting the gables, and lancet-shaped windows. The house has at times been known as the Pink Cottage, on account of its distinctive color. The interior features Gothic furniture which dates to the 1840s. It also has some late-Victorian decorative features such as embossed Lincrusta-Walton wall covering, boldly patterned wall-to-wall carpeting, stained-glass windows, and Rococo-Revival rosewood furniture, so very popular in the 1880s.

The 3,000-square-foot garden is in the same pattern used in the 1850s,

ROSELAND COTTAGE

Courtesy of Historic New England

with twenty-one floral beds framed by boxwood and containing four thousand annuals. The garden has a small summer house that is reminiscent of a diminutive Greek temple. Another outbuilding is the carriage house, which, interestingly, has the oldest surviving indoor bowling alley in America. President Ulysses S. Grant bowled here!

MAINE

Blaine House

192 State Street
Augusta, ME 04332
Phone: 207-287-2301
www.blainehouse.org

"Dirigo—I lead"

—THE MOTTO OF THE STATE OF MAINE

As the official residence of the Governor of Maine, Blaine House is both a home and a house museum. It was built in 1833 for Captain James Hall. Some thirty years later, it was bought by James Gillespie Blaine (1830–1893). Blaine successively served as a US Congressman, Speaker of the House, US Senator, and Secretary of State. In 1884 he won the Republican nomination for the presidency of the United States but narrowly lost to Grover Cleveland. Blaine bought this house as a gift to his wife while serving in the Maine House of Representatives. They had the house enlarged, adding a mirror-image wing identical to the original house. Some interior walls were removed to enlarge the rooms to accommodate large parties. In 1919 Blaine's daughter Harriet Blaine Beal (1871–1958) gifted it to the people of Maine. Noted Maine architect John Calvin Stevens (1855–1940) remodeled the house with another addition. Today it is a rambling white building, its two hipped roofs crowned with Italianate cupolas. Stevens had designed more than one thousand houses and public buildings in Maine, and his fortes were the Colonial Revival and Shingle styles. After Stevens's work was done in 1921, Blaine House became the Executive Mansion.

A tour of Blaine House covers the blue and gold State Reception Room, which reflects the colors of Maine's flag. The mantels are Italian marble, and there are several oil paintings depicting Maine scenes. The State Dining Room has a green and silver color scheme, a reference to Maine's trees and lakes. The sterling silver service was salvaged from the battleship *Maine* which was sunk in Havana harbor in 1898, signaling the start of the Spanish-American War.

Secretary Blaine's study has the desk and chair he used while he was a Senator. Abraham Lincoln was President when fellow Republican

James G. Blaine was in the House of Representatives, and there are three Lincoln connections in the study. The first is the wallpaper. Chosen by Blaine, it replicates the paper in Lincoln's White House study. Over the mantel there is an engraving of the President. And on the desk there is a card that was presented to Blaine and signed "A. Lincoln."

The Sun Room occupies the former site of an open porch. The Family Dining Room is lit by a Waterford crystal chandelier, and a door from this room leads to the Governor's Garden, originally designed by the Olmsted brothers in 1929 (see page 64).

Olson House

Hathorne Point Road
Cushing, ME 04563
Phone: 207-596-6457
www.farnsworthmuseum.org

"I just couldn't get away from there . . . I'd always seem to gravitate back to the house."

—ANDREW WYETH

At first glance, the Olson House may seem uninspiring and nondescript: a saltwater farmhouse in a field, with no architectural details to distinguish it from so many similar houses. And yet it is an American icon. It and a young lady lying in the field before it are the subject of a tempera painting by Andrew Wyeth (1917-2009), *Christina's World*. Painted in 1948, it is one of about three hundred works Wyeth created during his summers in Cushing from 1939 to 1968. Wyeth had a studio in this house. When not here, he would work at his home in Chadds Ford, Pennsylvania. In recognition of his work, Andrew Wyeth was awarded the National Medal of Arts in 2007, two years before his death.

The young lady in the painting is Anna Christina Olson (1893–1968). She and her brother Alvaro lived in this, a late-eighteenth-century dwelling built by their ancestor Captain Samuel Hathorn II. *Christina's World* is in the collection of New York's Museum of Modern Art.

Woodlawn

Route 172
19 Black House Drive
Ellsworth, ME 04605
Phone: 201-667-8671
https://woodlawnmuseum.com

Woodlawn, also known as the Black House, is a dignified Federal-style mansion built between 1824 and 1827 on a 180-acre estate. The builder, John Black, was the first of three successive generations to live here. At first a year-round home, it became a summer house in 1874. The last family member to live here was George Nixon Black Jr. (1842–1928) who willed the property, the park, the gardens, and the house and all its contents to the Hancock County Trustees of Public Reservations.

Philadelphia bricks were used to construct Woodlawn. The house has a hipped roof and seven chimneys. The porch, balustrades, and the trim have Greek Revival details. All the objects housed here are original to the house and the family: portraits, photographs, and miniatures; American and European furniture; glassware, china, books, and nineteenth-century carpeting. The carriage barn and sleigh barn have original pieces.

Woodlawn Park features gardens, wide fields, orchards, a lily pond, a first-class croquet court, and two miles of wooded trails used for walking and running in warmer weather and snowshoeing and cross-country skiing in winter.

McLellan-Sweat Mansion

Portland Museum of Art
7 Congress Street
Portland, ME 04101
Phone: 207-775-6148
www.portlandmuseum.org

English settlers founded Portland in 1632, though it had several different names between then and 1786, when it was named after the Isle of Portland in Devonshire, England. When Maine separated from Massachusetts in 1820, Portland became its capital and remained so until 1832. A fire devastated the city on July 4, 1866, but it rebuilt and grew. In addition to fishing and shipping, Portland became a major shipbuilding center during both world wars. Beautifully sited on two peninsulas, Portland overlooks Casco Bay and its islands and today is enjoying a resurgence and renewal.

At first glance it may appear that the McLellan-Sweat Mansion was attached to the Portland Museum of Art, when in fact the opposite is true. This Federal-style brick house was constructed in 1800-1801 for shipping merchant Major Hugh McLellan (1758–1823) at a cost of $20,000. The architect was John Kimball Sr. (1758–1831). In 1880 Congressman Lorenzo de Medici Sweat (1818–1898) bought the house, and then in 1908 his widow donated it to the Portland Society of Art, today known as the Portland Museum of Art. The mansion became the museum, and in 1911 the beaux-arts L. D. M. Sweat Memorial Galleries were built and attached. The Charles Shipman Payson Building was added to that in 1981, using the plans of Henry Nichols Cobb of I. M. Pei and Partners. The museum's collection has over fifteen thousand fine and decorative art pieces, European and American, from the eighteenth century to the present. Works by Winslow Homer, Rodin, Degas, Monet, Picasso, Hassam, Lane, N. C. Wyeth, Sargent, Prendergast, Cezanne, Chagall, Daumier, and many others are on display. A recent acquisition is Winslow Homer's studio and home (see page 42).

The McLellan-Sweat Mansion has a granite foundation, with red-brick walls laid in a Flemish bond. Before the front door, there is a semi-circular portico with Doric columns. The 5,000-square-foot interior has a wide central hall which leads to a grand staircase. The house has been restored and was reopened to the public in 2002.

VICTORIA MANSION

Andrew Davis photo courtesy of

Victoria Mansion

Victoria Mansion

109 Danforth Street
Portland, ME 04101
Phone: 207-772-4841
www.victoriamansion.org

Victoria Mansion is named for Queen Victoria, but this was not always so. It was first named the Morse-Libby House. Ruggles Sylvester Morse (1816–1893), a native of Maine, made a fortune as a hotelier in Boston, New York, and New Orleans. He commissioned this summer home in 1858, and it was completed two years later. The architect was Henry Austin (1804–1891), who used the Italianate style. In 1845 Queen Victoria and Prince Albert had Osborne House built on the Isle of Wight. The queen and her consort chose the Italianate style in imitation of villas and farmhouses in Tuscany. Thereafter this style became very popular in Britain and America in the 1850s and 1860s. Some features of Italianate buildings include a large central tower, low-pitched roofs, large eaves with decorative pediments under them, and round-top windows and doors.

Ruggles Morse died in 1893. The house was then sold to J. R. Libby, whose family lived there until 1928. Damaged in the Great Hurricane of 1938, the house faced an uncertain future and possible demolition. (There were plans to put a gas station on the site.) Instead, William H. Holmes bought the house in 1941, re-named it the Victoria Mansion, and opened it to the public for tours.

The interior of Victoria Mansion may best be described as sumptuous. The palatial decor is the work of German-born designer Gustave Herter (1830–1898) and features the finest Victorian furniture, stained glass, gas lighting fixtures, large mirrors, decorative plaster, trompe l'oeil murals, and china and crystal.

Wadsworth-Longfellow House

489 Congress Street
Portland, ME 04101
Phone: 207-774-1822
www.hwlongfellow.org

"The lamps are lit, the fires burn bright. The house is full of life and light."

—HENRY WADSWORTH LONGFELLOW

Henry Wadsworth Longfellow (1807–1882) lived in this house for thirty-five years. He was born in his aunt's house nearby, and when he was eight months old his family moved here. Longfellow is best known and loved for his poems, among them "Evangeline," "The Song of Hiawatha," and "Paul Revere's Ride." But he was more than a poet. He was an educator, having taught at his alma mater, Bowdoin College, and at Harvard College (see page 69). He was also a novelist, essayist, and translator.

This house was lived in by four generations of the Wadsworth-Longfellow family. Revolutionary War General Peleg Wadsworth (1748–1829) built it in 1785. At first it was a two-story dwelling with a gambrel roof. When the general retired to the country, his daughter Zilpah, her husband Stephen Longfellow IV, and their children continued to live here. Following an 1814 house fire, the renovations included the addition of a third story. The last family member to live here was Anne Longfellow Pierce. When she died in 1901 she left the house and all its contents to the Maine Historical Society.

The Wadsworth-Longfellow House has the distinction of being the first brick house in Portland, the oldest existing structure on the Portland peninsula, and Maine's first house museum. Tours of the house encompass the front hall, the parlor, the parlor chamber, the sitting room, the sitting room chamber, the summer dining room, the kitchen, the kitchen chamber, and Annie's chamber. When the family lived here, there were vegetable gardens and fruit trees. Today there is a flower garden, which was created in 1924 and replanted in 2007.

Winslow Homer Studio and Home

Portland Museum of Art

7 Congress Street

Portland, ME 04101

Phone: 207-775-6148

www.portlandmuseum.org

"[Winslow Homer is] in a place by himself as the most original and one of the strongest of American painters."

—CONTEMPORARY CRITIQUE IN THE *NEW YORK EVENING POST*

Winslow Homer (1836–1910) is widely regarded as one of the finest artists America has ever produced. Descended from an old New England family, Homer was born in Boston in 1836. In his late teens he began his career in art as an apprentice in a lithography shop. He later became an illustrator, working mainly for *Harper's Weekly,* depicting Civil War scenes. As an artist he produced oil paintings, watercolors, drawings, and wood engravings depicting a wide spectrum of subjects: Americans at work and at leisure; subjects from his travels to Cuba, the Caribbean islands, the Adirondacks, Canada, Florida and other locales; children at play; the ocean and "those who go down to the sea in ships and do their business in the great waters" (Psalm 107). In 1883 Homer's family brought an estate at Prouts Neck in Scarborough. Winslow claimed the 1,500-square-foot carriage house as his and had it remodeled by architect John Calvin Stevens. The studio is just seventy-five feet from the ocean, and from his second floor "piazza" (porch) visitors may enjoy beautiful vistas, as Homer did. Here he lived and worked for the rest of his life, painting the sea and episodes from the lives of those who labored on it. He became a "Hermit with a brush," a "Yankee Robinson Crusoe cloistered on his art island." In 1908, Homer wrote to his sister: "All is lovely outside my house and inside of my house and myself." Two years later he died here and was buried at Mt. Auburn Cemetery in Cambridge, Massachusetts.

The studio remained in Winslow's family until 2006, when it was bought by the Portland Museum of Art. After extensive and thought-

WINSLOW HOMER
STUDIO

*Copyright Portland Museum of
Art, Maine*

ful restoration of the property, Winslow Homer's Studio was opened for tours in 2012.

Special note: All tours begin at the Portland Museum of Art, and reservations are required.

Hamilton House

40 Vaughan's Lane
South Berwick, ME 03908
Phone: 207-384-2454
www.historicnewengland.org/historic-properties/homes/
hamilton-house

Hamilton House sits on fifty acres perched above the Salmon Falls River, which borders New Hampshire. This was an ideal locale for the dock of merchant and Revolutionary War privateer Jonathan Hamilton (1745–1802). Built in the late 1780s for Hamilton, the house was sold by his heirs to a farming family, the Goodwins, in 1815. Because of time, nature, and neglect, the house deteriorated. In 1898, neighbor Sarah Orne Jewett (see page 46) suggested that her friend Emily Tyson and Tyson's stepdaughter Elise Tyson Vaughan buy the house for use as a summer home. The ladies restored the house, updated it, and made it a Colonial Revival showpiece. They built a cottage which is now the visitor center and planted a perennial garden. Elise died in 1949, leaving the property to the Society for the Preservation of New England Antiquities (Historic New England today).

This two-and-a-half-story white Georgian house has a hip roof and four brick chimneys. In 1900 the walls of the wide central hall were hung with wallpaper that reproduced the original, and artist George Porter Fernald painted beautiful scenic wallpapers for the south parlor and dining room walls. Hamilton House is furnished with antique furniture and other pieces collected by Emily and Elise.

Sarah Orne Jewett House

5 Portland Street
South Berwick, ME 03908
Phone: 207-384-2454
www.historicnewengland.org/historic-properties/homes/
sarah-orne-jewett-house

Sarah Orne Jewett (1849–1909) was the author of novels, short stories, and poems. Her works can best be described as "American literary regionalism," since she wrote about what she knew and loved the most: the immediate area, its houses, its people, its history, and its distinctive charm.

This house was built at the bustling intersection of two main roads in 1774 for merchant John Haggins. After Haggins died in 1819 the house was lived in by the family of another merchant, Theodore Jewett. Jewett bought the house in 1839. The Jewetts were a growing family. Sarah Orne was born here in 1849, and in 1854 the Greek Revival Jewett Eastman House (the visitor center now) was built next door. Generations of the Jewetts and Eastmans lived in both houses. In the 1880s Sarah and her sister Mary updated the interior of the old family homestead to reflect current tastes, repapering the walls of the central hall and carpeting the main stairs with a runner designed by Englishman William Morris (1834–1896), a leader in the late-nineteenth-century Arts and Crafts movement. Sarah Orne Jewett died in 1909, and in 1931 her nephew donated the property to the Society for the Preservation of New England Antiquities.

Sayward-Wheeler House

9 Barrell Lane Extension
York Harbor, ME 03911
Phone: 207-384-2454
www.historicnewengland.org/historic-properties/homes/
sayward-wheeler-house

Captain John Smith explored this area in 1614 and named it Agamenticus. In 1641 it became the first English city chartered in the Americas. No longer a city, the town of York, named for York, England, is known for its colonial sites, beaches, and picturesque waterways. One of these waterways is the York River, which the Sayward-Wheeler House overlooks. The house was built about 1718 and bought in 1735 by Jonathan Sayward (1713–1797), a judge, merchant, and Tory. In the 1760s he had the house enlarged, embellished, and furnished with finer pieces. He was revered by his family, and after his death his descendants preserved the house as it was when he was alive. Consequently this is one of the best-preserved colonial interiors in the nation. This house was shown to visitors as a museum as early as the 1860s.

In 1900 a grandson (Sayward Barrel) sold the house and its contents to another descendant, Elizabeth Cheever Wheeler. She made some changes, added plumbing and electricity, painted some of the interior white, and added new wallpapers. But the original furnishings, portraits, and other decor remained. This was used as a summer home until 1977, when it was given to the SPNEA.

MASSACHUSETTS

DAGUERREOTYPE OF
EMILY DICKINSON
ABOUT 1847
Courtesy of Amherst College
Archives

Emily Dickinson Museum

280 Main Street

Amherst, MA 01002

Phone: 413-542-8161

www.emilydickinsonmuseum.org

"I'm Nobody! Who are you?

Are you—Nobody—too?

Then there's a pair of us!

Don't tell! They'd advertise—you know!

"How dreary—to be—Somebody!

How public—like a Frog—

To tell one's name—the lifelong June—

To an admiring Bog!"

—EMILY DICKINSON

This area was settled by the British in the 1730s. Amherst was incorporated in 1776 and was named for Baron Jeffrey Amherst, a British commander during the French and Indian War. In 1821 Amherst College was established, and one of its founders was Samuel Fowler Dickinson (1775–1838), grandfather to Emily Dickinson (1830–1886).

The Emily Dickinson Museum comprises two houses. The first is the Homestead. Built for Samuel Fowler Dickinson in 1813, granddaughter Emily was born here in 1830. She lived in this house nearly all her life. A recluse, Emily preferred to stay at the Homestead. As she grew older, she cherished her solitude more and more, to the point where she refused to see visitors or even, later in life, to leave her room. After her death, Emily's younger sister Lavinia discovered, hidden in a locked chest in Emily's bedroom, a collection of nearly 1,800 poems she had written.

The Homestead was bought by Emily's father, Edward, in 1830. The last Dickinson to live here was Lavinia, who bequeathed the house to her niece Martha Dickinson Bianchi. It was rented to tenants, then sold to another family, who in turn sold it to the Trustees of Amherst College in 1965. It then became a museum.

The Homestead was built in the then popular Federal style. As the colors of the bricks varied, the house was painted a uniform red. By the 1830s tastes had changed, and the house was transformed into a Greek Revival dwelling: The roof was raised, a gabled roof replaced a hip roof, and the house was painted white. In 1855 this home was enlarged with the addition of a new kitchen and laundry wing, a conservatory, a veranda, and an Italianate cupola atop the roof.

The second house at the museum, The Evergreens, which Edward built in 1856 for his son (and Emily's brother) Austin, is next door. It was a wedding gift. Austin's daughter, Martha Dickinson Bianchi, lived here until she died in 1943, preserving the interior as she had inherited it, complete with original furniture, family heirlooms, artwork, wallcoverings, books, fabrics, and other objects. It then also became a museum. The Homestead and The Evergreens united to become the Emily Dickinson Museum in 2003.

Austin Dickinson was a friend and associate of the great landscape architect Frederick Law Olmsted (see page 64). Much of the landscaping here is the work of Olmsted: native and exotic trees and shrubbery, and areas of lawn and open space.

Isabella Stewart Gardner Museum

25 Evans Way
Boston, MA 02115
Phone: 617-566-1401
www.gardnermuseum.org

*"... I decided that the greatest need in our Country was art ... we
were a very young country and had very few opportunities of seeing
beautiful things, works of art ... So I determined to make it my life's
work if I could."*

—ISABELLA STEWART GARDNER

For a bit of Venice (and a lot of Europe) in Boston, visit the Gardner
Museum. Isabella Stewart Gardner (1840–1924) was an heiress,
philanthropist, patron of the arts, and avid art collector. When she came
into her inheritance upon her father's death in 1891, she began to work
with art historian and collector Bernard Berenson (1865–1959) to acquire
dozens of Old Master paintings. In 1898 she bought this property and
hired architect Willard T. Sears (1837–1920) to create a Venetian palace
to be both her home and her museum. Its model and inspiration was the
Palazzo Barbaro. Built in 1425, the Venetian Gothic palace on the Grand
Canal had become the nucleus of the Barbaro Circle: a group of American artists and patrons that included Gardner, Berenson, James McNeill
Whistler, John Singer Sargent, Edith Wharton, Henry James, and others.
They would be very much at home here at Fenway Court, as Mrs. Gardner
named her palazzo.

The three-story house and museum are built around a central garden
courtyard, which is protected by a glass roof. All year round, the garden
is abloom with changing floral displays. Mrs. Jack (as Mrs. Gardner was
often called) toured Europe and collected ancient architectural fittings,
sculptures, columns, and capitals to be incorporated into her museum.
She personally chose the more than 2,500 artworks in her collection:
paintings, sculptures, furniture, drawings, illuminated manuscripts,
books, ceramics, silver, fabrics, and letters. The collection reached as far
back as ancient times and spanned Europe, Asia, the Islamic world, and
contemporary America. Artists represented include Rembrandt, Michel-

angelo, Botticelli, Raphael, Titian, Sargent, Whistler, Degas, and Manet. Isabella herself arranged the display of everything in her museum. It was opened to the public on New Year's Day 1903 to the sounds of the Boston Symphony Orchestra.

When Mrs. Gardner died in 1924, she left her museum and a $1 million endowment "for the education and enjoyment of the public forever." In accordance with her wishes, an Anglican Mass is sung for the repose of her soul annually in Fenway Court's chapel. She also stipulated that were any part of her museum to be changed in any way, it and its contents are to be sold and the proceeds given to Harvard University.

A grim chapter in the history of Fenway Court occurred the night of March 18, 1990 when two men disguised as police officers broke into the museum and stole thirteen works of art. The total value of these is $500 million—the costliest property theft ever to occur anywhere in the world. To date, the case has not been solved nor the works recovered. Empty picture frames hang on the walls where the paintings once were.

In 2012, a new wing was added to the Gardner Museum, designed by Italian architect Renzo Piano (b. 1937). It stands on the site of the former stables and includes a new entrance, visitor center, restaurant, shop, reading room, concert hall, and space for special exhibits and programs. Strikingly modern, the cost of construction was $118 million. From here visitors reach the palazzo by way of a long corridor that may be thought of as a time tunnel, linking the twenty-first century to the fifteenth.

The Nichols House Museum

55 Mount Vernon Street
Boston, MA 02108
Phone: 617-227-6993
www.nicholshousemuseum.org

Beacon Hill as we know it today was leveled and developed around 1800 by the Mount Vernon Proprietors. At first this was a steeper hill on top of which a beacon or light on a pole was lit to signal emergencies to the townsfolk. The beacon pole stood from 1634 to 1789, hence the name of the hill.

This is a design by the prolific Boston architect Charles Bulfinch (1763–1844). One of the first houses on Beacon Hill, this four-story town house was completed in 1804 for politician Jonathan Mason. The house was renovated in 1830 and bought by Dr. Arthur Nichols (1840–1923) in 1885.

Dr. Nichols' eldest daughter, Rose Standish Nichols (1872–1960), would live here for the rest of her life, inheriting it in 1935. Miss Nichols was the first American woman to be a landscape architect and wrote several books on the subject. She was a skilled embroiderer, furniture maker, and wood carver, and her work is on display here. Miss Nichols was a pacifist, a strong supporter of women's suffrage, and a member of the Cornish Art Colony in New Hampshire, as was Augustus Saint-Gaudens (see page 144). When she died he willed that her family's home be opened as a museum.

The only house museum on the Hill, the Nichols House presents the material surroundings of a Beacon Hill upper-class family during the last two centuries. The European and American furniture dates from the 1600s to the twentieth century, and the art collection contains sculptures by Saint-Gaudens; other American, European, and Asian art; portraits; Flemish tapestries; and other family possessions.

Gibson House Museum

137 Beacon Street
Boston, MA 02116
Phone: 617-267-6338
www.thegibsonhouse.org

"[Beacon Street is] the sunny street that holds the sifted few."

—OLIVER WENDELL HOLMES SR.

The Boston neighborhood known as Back Bay rests on land that is man-made. The bay was filled in with gravel from suburban Needham, Massachusetts in 1857. Gibson House was one of the first townhouses to be built in the newly created neighborhood. The property had been bought by a widow, Catherine Hammond Gibson, and architect Edward Clarke Cabot designed this Victorian row house in the Italian Renaissance style, using red brick and brownstone for the building materials.

This was home to three generations of the Gibson family. Mrs. Gibson passed the house to her son Charles Hammond Gibson, who in turn passed it to his son Charles Jr. Charles died in 1954, stipulating that it be opened to the public as a museum. Gibson House is significant in that it is an intact Victorian house with original family furnishings, artifacts, and decor.

The first floor entrance walls are covered with "Japanese leather," a heavily embossed paper that resembles tooled leather. The arches and woodwork are black walnut. In the dining room the table is set for a formal dinner. The second floor has a central hall flanked by two parlors: one serves as the music room and the other is the library. Above that are two bedrooms, a dressing room, and a bath with fixtures dating to 1902. The house tour ends on the ground floor, where the laundry room, kitchen, pantry, and coal shed are located.

OTIS HOUSE

Courtesy of Historic New

England

Otis House

141 Cambridge Street
Boston, MA 02114
Phone: 617-994-5920
www.historicnewengland.org/historic-properties/homes/
otis-house

This is the first of three Boston houses built for Harrison Gray Otis (1765–1884). All three are red-brick mansions designed by Bostonian Charles Bulfinch (1763–1844) in the Federal style. The second (built in 1802) stands at 85 Mount Vernon Street, the third (1806) at 45 Beacon Street (now the headquarters for the American Meteorological Society). Of the three, only the Otis House is a museum.

Harrison Gray Otis was a notable figure in Boston. An attorney, congressman, and Boston mayor, he was also one of the Mount Vernon Proprietors who developed a large portion of Beacon Hill at the start of the nineteenth century. Portraits of Mr. and Mrs. Otis by Gilbert Stuart (1755–1828) hang in the house.

After Otis moved on to house number two, this house had a series of owners, and it was used successively as a private home, a clinic, apartments, a "genteel" boarding house, and by 1868, a rooming house. The Society for the Preservation of New England Antiquities (now Historic New England) bought the house in 1916 and restored it. In 1925 Cambridge Street was widened, threatening Otis House. To avoid demolition the house was moved back forty feet and is now attached to two pre-existing row houses on Lynde Street.

This is a three-story mansion, five bays across. Above the front door is a Palladian window, and above that there is a lunette window. The interior has been thoughtfully restored in the style of Robert Adam (1728–1792), an English architect who favored and promoted neoclassical design and furniture.

The Paul Revere House

19 North Square
Boston, MA 02113
Phone: 617-523-2338
www.paulreverehouse.org

"Listen my children and you shall hear
Of the midnight ride of Paul Revere,
On the 18th of April, in seventy-five;
Hardly a man is now alive
Who remembers that famous day and year."

—HENRY WADSWORTH LONGFELLOW, "PAUL REVERE'S RIDE"

Of all the house museums in Boston, this undoubtedly is the best known and most visited. Aside from its association with one of America's great Patriots, the house is notable in that it is the oldest house in downtown Boston. It was built in about 1680 for Robert Howard, a successful merchant. Paul Revere (1735–1818) bought the house in 1770 and lived here with his two wives (he remarried after the death of the first) and as many as nine of his sixteen children. Revere supported his family as a successful silversmith and engraver of prints. Some of his work is on display at the Museum of Fine Arts in Boston. Born in this neighborhood, the North End, he was the son of Apollos Rivoire, a French Huguenot. Paul Revere was immortalized by his midnight ride on April 18, 1775.

Revere sold this house in 1800. The building was then used variously as tenements, a candy store, a fruit and vegetable store, a bank, and a cigar factory. Threatened with demolition in 1902, the house was bought by Paul Revere's great-grandson, John P. Reynolds Jr. It was restored to its original and present appearance by the preservationist architect Joseph Chandler (1864–1945). Opened to the public in 1908, this was one of the first historic house museums in America.

Ninety percent of the structure of this three-story L-shaped house is original. The interior has the heavy beams and large fireplaces so typical of houses of this period. Two bedrooms have some furniture which belonged to Revere.

THE PAUL REVERE

HOUSE

Zack Frank / Shutterstock.com

Behind the Revere House, there is a visitor and education center in which there are two floors of exhibits. Next door is the early Georgian Pierce-Hichborn House, which dates to about 1711. Both houses and the visitor and education center are operated by the Paul Revere Memorial Association.

William Hickling Prescott House

55 Beacon Street
Boston, MA 02108
Phone: 617-742-3190
http://nscdama.org/william-hickling-prescott-house/

This townhouse is the 1808 work of Benjamin Asher (1773–1845). A champion of the Federal and Greek Revival styles, Asher wrote seven books on architectural design which became widely read and used through much of this country.

This house was built for James Smith Colburn (1780–1859), and it was attached to an adjoining twin town house mansion of the same design. Both houses were free-standing when built and had water views, as the Back Bay and what would become the Boston Public Garden had not been filled in. William Hickling Prescott (1796–1859) bought the house in 1845. One of the first historians in America, his expertise was Spanish history. He wrote books on late-Renaissance Spain and the early Spanish empire in the Americas. Prescott died in this house in 1859. His widow sold the house to cousins, the Dexters. In 1944 the property was acquired by the Massachusetts chapter of the National Society of the Colonial Dames of America. This is also known as Headquarters House.

The red-brick house is four stories high, and the facade has a distinctive round bay framed by pilasters. The elegant interior includes Prescott's study, which has been meticulously and accurately restored by the Colonial Dames.

Frederick Law Olmsted National Historic Site

99 Warren Street
Brookline, MA 02445
Phone: 617-566-1689
www.nps.gov/frla/

> *"An artist, he paints with lakes and wooded slopes; with lawns and banks*
> *and forest covered hills; with mountain sides and ocean views."*
>
> —DANIEL BURNHAM

Frederick Law Olmsted (1822–1903) was many things: a conservationist, a public administrator, and a social critic. But he is best known as the father of American landscape architecture. His most renowned work is Central Park in Manhattan, but he created a lot more. His favorite park was Prospect Park in Brooklyn, New York. His parks, academic campuses, and other landscape works across the country—as far away as San Francisco—would be too numerous to recount here. But in the Boston area, his major contribution was the design of the Emerald Necklace, a series of open spaces, green areas, and parks linked by waterways and parkways. The Emerald Necklace starts with the Boston Common (1634) and the Boston Public Garden (1837); continues down the mall of Commonwealth Avenue; then on to the Fens (past the Gardner Museum—see page 53), the Riverway, Olmsted Park, Jamaica Pond, the Jamaicaway, the Arborway, and the Arnold Arboretum; and ends at Franklin Park.

Olmsted frequently worked with the great American architect Henry Hobson Richardson (1838–1886). Richardson lived in Brookline and suggested that Olmsted do the same. So in 1883 Olmsted (whose name means "place of the elm") bought Fairsted, an 1810 Federal farmhouse built for the Clark family. Once there, Olmsted and his son John Charles landscaped the property and renovated the house. In 1903 a wing was added for the landscaping firm. And so this site presents a home, an office, and a garden.

After Olmsted died, his sons Frederick Jr. and John Charles continued in their father's footsteps. The firm became known as the Olmsted Brothers company. The Olmsted family lived here until 1936, when they rented the house to others while maintaining the company's office here. The business closed in 1980, and the property was sold to the National Park Service, which now offers tours. The house exterior has been restored, as has the garden. Within, the house's original wall coverings have been reproduced, and there are displays of photographs of the house interior as it was in Olmsted's time. The part of the site used by the Olmsted Brothers company has archives and storage space for more than one hundred thousand documents used on about five thousand projects, as well as photos, models, tools, and work space. The work of Olmsted and his sons' firm is well documented and presented here.

John Fitzgerald Kennedy National Historic Site

83 Beals Street
Brookline, MA 02446
Phone: 617-566-7937
www.nps.gov/jofi/index.htm

"Life isn't a matter of milestones, but of moments."

—ROSE FITZGERALD KENNEDY

It was here that the nation's thirty-fifth president was born on May 29, 1917. This suburban house was built in 1909 and bought by Joseph and Rose Kennedy at the time of their marriage in 1915. The family grew, and they sold this house and moved into a larger one in 1920.

In 1966, three years after the president's assassination, the Kennedy family repurchased this house. Rose Kennedy had the house restored to what it was when Jack Kennedy was born here. About 20 percent of the furnishings are original, and the balance of furniture and objects is true to the period and nearly duplicates what was here previously. Rose Kennedy donated the house to the National Park Service in 1967, and it has been open to the public for tours ever since.

A visit to the house begins in the basement. What was once the laundry room is now the visitor center, with an introductory film, exhibits, and a shop. On the first floor, the parlor has the piano that was given as a wedding gift to Rose and Joseph. In the dining room the table is set with Rose's wedding china. The second floor is where visitors may see the master bedroom in which the president was born. His sisters Rose and Kathleen were also born in this room. Next door is the girls' bedroom. The boudoir was Rose's private domain and work space.

The tour includes a glimpse of the servants' work area in the kitchen. Their living quarters on the third floor are now used as offices by NPS staff. The National Park Service offers walking tours of the neighborhood, where participants see sites familiar to Jack during his boyhood in Brookline.

LONGFELLOW HOUSE-
WASHINGTON'S
HEADQUARTERS

Courtesy National Park Service,
Longfellow House-Washington's
Headquarters National Historic
Site

Longfellow House-Washington's Headquarters

National Historic Site
105 Brattle Street
Cambridge, MA 02138
Phone: 617-876-4491
www.nps.gov/long/index.htm

"Stay, stay at home, my heart and rest;
Home-keeping hearts are the happiest,
For those that wonder they know not where
Are full of trouble and full of care;
To stay at home is best."

—HENRY WADSWORTH LONGFELLOW

This stately Georgian mansion was home to both a president and a poet. The story begins in 1759 when the house was built for John Vassal. He was a Tory, and when the British evacuated Boston he also left.

General George Washington made the Vassal House his home and headquarters during the siege of Boston from July 1775 to April 1776. Martha Washington joined him here for a time.

Following the Washingtons, there were several occupants. In 1791 Andrew Craigie, who served under Washington as Apothecary General of the Army, bought the house. After his death in 1819 his widow Elizabeth Craigie began to take in boarders. One boarder was Henry Wadsworth Longfellow (1807–1882), who at that time was a Harvard professor.

Elizabeth Craigie died in 1841. Two years later Longfellow married Frances (Fanny) Appleton. Her father purchased this house and presented it to them as a wedding gift. The poet would live in this house until his death. Here he wrote some of his best and most-loved poems, including "The Song of Hiawatha," "Evangeline," "The Courtship of Miles Standish," "Paul Revere's Ride," and "The Village Blacksmith."

Tragically, Fanny died in this house in 1861 after her dress caught fire. Longfellow died in 1882. His descendants preserved the house and donated it to the National Park Service in 1972.

The house interior looks just as it did when Longfellow lived here: historic furnishings and decorative arts; a library of ten thousand books; paintings by artists such as Jacques Louis David, Albert Bierstadt, and Jean-Baptiste-Camille Corot; Japanese and Chinese art and artifacts; and manuscript and archives collections. The garden has recently been restored, and beyond the front door, Longfellow Park stretches to the Charles River. It contains the Longfellow Memorial, the work of Daniel Chester French (see page 130) and Henry Bacon—the same men who collaborated on the creation of the Lincoln Memorial in Washington, DC.

Ralph Waldo Emerson House

28 Cambridge Turnpike
Concord, MA 01742
Phone: 978-369-2236
www.nps.gov/nr/travel/massachusetts_conservation/
ralph_waldo_emerson_house

"The ornament of a house is the friends who frequent it."

—RALPH WALDO EMERSON

Ralph Waldo Emerson (1803–1882) was a poet, philosopher, essayist, lecturer, and transcendentalist. This house was built in 1828, and in 1835 Emerson wrote, "I bought my house and two acres six rods of land of John T. Coolidge for 3,500 dollars." The house had been known as Coolidge Castle, but Emerson christened it Bush. He would live and write here the rest of his life. Emerson lived with his wife and mother; Henry David Thoreau also lived with them for a time.

Bush eventually went to the Emersons' son Edward, who lived here until his death in 1930. It was then acquired by the Ralph Waldo Emerson Memorial Association, which maintains the house as a museum. The interior is as it was save for Emerson's study, which is in the Concord Museum just across the road at 53 Cambridge Turnpike. Visitors are welcome to tour the garden. The meadow walk retraces Emerson's steps to Mill Brook.

Louisa May Alcott's Orchard House

399 Lexington Road
Concord, MA 01702
Phone: 978-369-4118
www.louisamayalcott.org

"Tis a pretty retreat and ours; a family mansion to take pride in . . ."

—AMOS BRONSON ALCOTT

W hen founded in 1635, Concord was the first inland Puritan settle-ment. Initially known as Musketaquid, the name Concord was later adopted to reflect the peaceful coexistence between the local Indi-ans and the English settlers. Concord is best known for the "shot heard round the world," the beginning of the American Revolution on April 19, 1775. In the nineteenth century the town became a haven for literati, philosophers, and artists, among them Louisa May Alcott, Ralph Waldo Emerson, Nathaniel Hawthorne, Henry David Thoreau, and sculptor Daniel Chester French, all of whose houses are featured in this book, and all of whom are buried at the Author's Ridge in Concord's Sleepy Hollow Cemetery (34A Bedford Street). Another Concord resident, Ephraim Bull, cultivated the first Concord grapes in 1850.

Louisa May Alcott (1832–1888), novelist and poet, lived here with her family for nineteen years starting in 1858. They first came to Concord in 1840. Three years later her father, Amos Bronson Alcott, moved the fam-ily to the town of Harvard, Massachusetts, where he founded Fruitlands (see page 92), a Utopian agrarian community. After the venture failed, the Alcotts returned to Concord two years later and bought Hillside, which was sold to Nathaniel Hawthorne in 1852 (see The Wayside, page 76).

The Alcotts—Bronson, his wife, Abigail May, and their daughters, Anna, Louisa, and May—made this place their home in 1858. There were two houses on the twelve-acre site, both dating to about 1690–1720. There was an orchard of forty apple trees, and so their home came to be named Orchard House. Bronson joined the two houses into one and set about making many improvements. As a friend, Lydia Maria Child (1802–1888), observed, "The result is a house full of queer nooks and corners and all manner of juttings in and out. It seems as if the spirit of some old architect

had brought it from the Middle Ages and dropped it down in Concord. . . . The whole house leaves a general impression of harmony, of a medieval sort."

One of the improvements was the shelf desk Bronson crafted for his daughter Louisa. Here in 1868 she wrote her most beloved novel, *Little Women*, which is set in Orchard House.

After Mrs. Alcott died in 1877, Louisa, her father, and her sister Anna moved to 255 Main Street in Concord, and in 1884 Orchard House was sold to a family friend, William Torrey Harris.

About three-quarters of the furnishings in Orchard House are Alcott family heirlooms. The rest are true to the period. Visitors tour the dining room, parlor, kitchen, study, and bedrooms. The property includes gardens as well as Mr. Alcott's Hillside Chapel.

The Old Manse

269 Monument Street

Concord, MA 01742

Phone: 978-369-3909

www.thetrustees.org/places-to-visit/greater-boston/old-manse

"Between two tall gateposts of roughhewn stone . . . we behold the gray front of the old parsonage, terminating the vista of an avenue of black ash trees."

—NATHANIEL HAWTHORNE

A "manse" by definition is a house lived in by a minister and his family. This Georgian clapboard manse was the home of the minister of Concord's First Parish Church. It was built in 1770 for the Reverend William Emerson (1743–1776) and his minister son, William Jr. (1769–1811). William Jr.'s son was Ralph Waldo Emerson (1803–1882), who stayed at the Manse in 1834. It was here that he wrote what is perhaps his best known work, his essay "Nature."

Another writer, Nathaniel Hawthorne (1804–1864), took up residence here in 1842. He and his artist wife Sophia Peabody (1809–1871) rented the house for $100 per annum. They lived here for three years. Henry David Thoreau cultivated a vegetable garden here for them. On a window pane, Hawthorne inscribed a poem, "composed by my wife and written with her diamond." It was in this house that Hawthorne wrote parts of "Mosses from an Old Manse." Unfortunately the Hawthornes were evicted from the Manse in 1845 for failure to pay their rent.

The house continued to be owned and lived in by Emerson descendants until 1939, when it went to The Trustees of Reservations, who maintain it as a museum. The interior is well preserved: woodwork, wall coverings, furniture, books, kitchen utensils, and many other items.

Visitors may walk through the property and see the orchard, the boathouse on the Concord River, and the North Bridge nearby.

The Wayside

455 Lexington Road
Concord, MA 01742
Phone: 978-318-7683
https://www.nps.gov/nr/travel/pwwmh/ma47.htm

"It does me very good to be alone, and Mother has made it pretty and neat for me."

—LOUISA MAY ALCOTT

At different times in its history, this house was home to three authors. The first was Louisa May Alcott (1832–1888). After a time at her father's Utopian community at Fruitlands (see page 92), the family returned to Concord and bought this house in 1845. It dates to 1717, though the first owner's name has been lost to history. We do know, however, that on April 19, 1775, resident and minuteman Samuel Whitely observed British troops marching by his door. Soon after, Professor John Winthop and his family lived in this house during the period when Harvard College classes were in Concord to escape the military hostilities in Cambridge.

The Alcotts named their home Hillside. It was originally a colonial saltbox house, but Amos expanded it. He cut the shed in two and attached the two halves to either side of the house, added more bedrooms including one for Louisa, and landscaped the property. Hillside, in part, became the inspiration for Louisa's best loved book, *Little Women*, which she later wrote at Orchard House (see page 72). The house also became a stop on the Underground Railroad.

The family's stay here was brief. Hillside was sold to Nathaniel Hawthorne for $1,500 in 1852. Mr. Hawthorne lived here with his wife and three children, renaming the property The Wayside. Regarding his new home, he wrote, " Mr. Alcott . . . had wasted a good deal of money in fitting it up to suit his own taste—all of which improvements I get for little or nothing. Having been much neglected, the place is the raggedest in the world but it will make, sooner or later, a comfortable and sufficiently pleasant home." In the 1860s he added his three-story writing tower and other rooms. But he was not entirely pleased with the end result. Wrote Hawthorne in 1864, "I have been equally unsuccessful in my architectural projects; and have transformed a simple and small farm-house into the absurdist anomaly you ever saw; but I really was not so much to blame here as the village-carpenter, who took the matter into his own hands, and produced an unimaginable sort of thing instead of what I asked for."

Six years after Hawthorne's death in 1864, his widow Sophia sold the house to her daughter Rose and Rose's husband George Parsons Lathrop, who in turn sold it in 1883 to Boston publisher Daniel Lathrop (1831–1892). Daniel's wife Harriet Lathrop (1844–1924) was a successful author. Under the pseudonym Margaret Sidney, she wrote a number of children's books. When Sidney died in 1924, the house was inherited by her daughter. This became a museum in 1927 and a property of the National Park Service in 1965. The house recently went through a thorough restoration, reopening for tours in 2016.

Thoreau Farm

341 Virginia Road
Concord, MA 01742
Phone: 978-451-0300
http://thoreaufarm.org/

"[I was] born July 12, 1817 in the Minot House, on the Virginia Road,

where Father occupied Grandmother's thirds, carrying on the farm."

—HENRY DAVID THOREAU

This house was built around 1730 for John Wheeler and was bought by Deacon Samuel Minot for his son Jonas. Jonas was the stepfather of Henry David Thoreau's mother. The Wheeler-Minot Farmhouse, as it is also known, is a wood-frame house standing two and a half stories high, with many common features of New England domestic architecture, including clapboard siding and a fieldstone foundation. The property was bought by the Thoreau Family Trust in 1995.

Henry David Thoreau (1817–1862) was a true son of Concord. Not only was he born here, but he also lived most of his life in the town. Thoreau was a poet, essayist, philosopher, abolitionist, naturalist, surveyor, and historian. His best known writings are his essay "Civil Disobedience" (1849) and his 1854 book *Walden*. Thoreau's retreat is open to visitors today as the Walden Pond State Reservation (915 Walden Street in Concord). It has a replica of Thoreau's cabin.

In *Walden*, Thoreau wrote, "I went to the woods because I wished to live deliberately, to front only the essential facts of life, and see if I could not learn what it had to teach, and not, when I came to die, discover that I had not lived."

RECONSTRUCTED CABIN

Alizada Studios /

Shutterstock.com

The Fairbanks House

511 East Street
Dedham, MA 02026
Phone: 781-326-1170
www.fairbankshouse.org

The Fairbanks House is a treasure. More than 380 years old, it is the oldest surviving timber-frame house in North America.

This dwelling was built in 1637 by a Puritan settler, Jonathan Fairebanke, from Yorkshire, England. In 1633 he migrated to Boston and from there moved inland to Dedham in 1636 or 1637. Here, Fairebanke lived with his wife Grace and their six children. It remained home to eight generations of the Fairbanks family. It is the oldest American house lived in continuously by the same family, all linear descendants. Today it is owned and operated by the Fairbanks Family in America.

The house was built around one large central chimney which was flanked by two large rooms on the first floor, two on the second, and an attic above. One room on the first floor was the hall, where meals were prepared and eaten. The other first-floor room was the parlor, which doubled as a sitting room and a bedroom.

Over the years, additions were made to the house. These and the original space are intact, reflecting different building styles.

Houses of Historic Deerfield

Old Main Street
Deerfield, MA 01342
Phone: 413-774-5581
www.historic-deerfield.org

When Deerfield was founded in 1669, it was a frontier town at the far northwestern reach of New England. Caught in the French and Indian War, it was twice devastated by Indian attacks: in 1675 at the Bloody Brook Massacre and again in 1704 at the Deerfield Raid, when the town was torched and burned. After the Treaty of Paris was signed in 1763, settlers began to rebuild. Deerfield Academy, a preparatory school, was founded in 1797. The mile-long Old Main Street (or simply "The Street") is lined with preserved, restored, and rebuilt eighteenth- and nineteenth-century homes and public buildings, many of which are open to visitors under the auspices of Historic Deerfield, an organization begun in 1948 by Henry and Helen Flynt. It has grown to include more than a dozen buildings and a collection of more than twenty-seven thousand objects. Begin with a visit to Hall Tavern Information Center, adjacent to Historic Deerfield's parking lot. Built in 1765 in Claremont, Massachusetts, the tavern was moved to this site in 1949.

In addition to Deerfield's house museums, there are three sites worth visiting in the village. The Flynt Center of Early New England Life is a modern, climate-controlled facility with exhibition galleries and visible storage areas. Memorial Hall Museum is in the Academy's early school building, which dates to 1798. It houses the Early American collection of architectural historian George Sheldon. The Henry Flynt Silver and Metalware Collection is on display. For a bite to eat, try the Deerfield Inn. And for a scenic walk to work off your lunch, amble along the Channing Blake Footpath.

Allen House

The Allen House dates to 1734. In 1945 it was renovated by Historic Deerfield founders Mr. and Mrs. Flynt. Their home is as they left it, with their personal collections.

VIEW OF SHELDON
HOUSE AND WILLIAMS
HOUSE, HISTORIC
DEERFIELD
Courtesy of Historic Deerfield,
photo by Penny Leveritt

Ashley House

This was the first house restored by Historic Deerfield in 1948. Built in the 1730s, it was the minister's house. In the 1750s the Reverend John Ashley had the house enlarged and improved. He added the kind of large, decorative door frame that was so typical of Connecticut River Valley buildings at that time. He also added a large central staircase in the hall and embellished the interior with fine paneling. Ashley House is furnished with period pieces: mahogany and cherry furniture and decorative objects.

Dwight House

Dwight House is unique in that it is one of only four houses in Deerfield that are not original to the town. It was built in Springfield, Massachusetts in 1754. Threatened with demolition in 1950, it was dismantled and brought here.

This is a charming, diminutive house with a gambrel roof and decorative pediments over the door and windows. It contains the Apprentice's Workshop, where visitors may try their hand at colonial crafts, such as the making of pottery, woodworking, and the weaving of fabrics.

Frary House

Frary House dates to about 1760. In 1892 it was bought by a schoolteacher, Miss C. Alice Baker. She restored the house and filled it with her collection of New England antiques, including furniture, wrought iron, baskets, needlework, and other crafts. In the late nineteenth century, following the National Centennial celebrations in 1876, there was a reawakening of interest in America's colonial past and its material culture. In architecture, this came to be expressed in Colonial Revival buildings. Miss Baker led the Colonial Revival movement in Deerfield, which in turn brought visitors to the town and an economic boost to the area.

Sheldon House

This was home to an extended family of farmers. This is a two-story house with one central chimney. Sheldon House was constructed in about 1757, and in 1802 an addition was made to the back to accommodate a growing family. The house is seen today as it might have been during the Federal era, from about 1780 to 1810, when three generations of the Sheldon family lived here.

Stebbins House

Asa Stebbins had this house built in 1799. He was a mill owner, a farmer, and one of Deerfield's wealthier citizens. This brick house is a departure from the many wood-frame houses in Deerfield, and it does not have the Connecticut River Valley "signature," a bold pediment over the front door. Both outside and in, this is a Federal period piece. The interior is richly decorated with French wallpaper of the period by Joseph Defour et Cie, depicting the three voyages of Captain Cook to the South Seas between 1769 and 1779. Other walls are painted with works attributed to Jared Jessup. One of many itinerant artists at that time, Jessup would travel from town to town and from door to door looking for commissions. The furnishings and accessories are true to the period, and there are several oil portraits.

Wells-Thorn House

This house was built in 1747, and the exterior was painted a distinct robin's-egg blue about 1803. The interior is not devoted to a single historic period, but to many periods. The first room is furnished as such a room would have been in 1725, when Deerfield was on the western frontier of Massachusetts. The rooms progress to later periods and culminate with the final one, which is furnished as it would have been in 1850, during the Antebellum period.

Williams House

This is a white clapboard house with a hipped roof and a fanlight over the front door. It dates to 1730, though the house's appearance today reflects the extensive renovations that were done in 1816. Ebenezer Hinsdale Williams was from Roxbury, Massachusetts. After graduating from Harvard College, he moved west to Deerfield, where he earned a living as a landowner and farmer. He lived here with his wife Anna and their two daughters. Some of the walls are covered with wallpaper imported from France which depicts scenes in Venice. Other papers are reproductions based on remnants of originals. The furniture and decor are from the Federal era.

Wright House

There are parallels between this house and the Stebbins House. Both are red-brick and in the Federal style. And both were built for a man named Asa Stebbins. The Stebbins House dates to 1799. Stebbins then built this house twenty-five years later in 1824 as a wedding gift for his son Asa Stebbins Jr., who was a farmer, the town treasurer, and a selectman. His descendants sold the house to George and Jane Wright in 1908. Then in 1948 it was sold to Henry and Helen Flynt, the founders of Historic Deerfield. The Wright House has galleries which are used for the display of Historic Deerfield's furniture collection. Special exhibits are mounted here periodically.

Cogswell's Grant

60 Spring Street
Essex, MA 01929
Phone: 978-768-3632
www.historicnewengland.org/historic-properties/homes/
cogswells-grant/cogswells-grant

This farm overlooking the scenic Essex River was the summer home of Bertram K. Little (1899–1993) and his wife Nina Fletcher Little (1903–1993). Their passion and area of expertise was American folk art. Mr. Little was the director of the Society for the Preservation of New England Antiquities from 1947 to 1970. Mrs. Little was a prolific writer on the subject of American folk art, writing books and articles.

The property originally was owned by John Cogswell (1592–1669), and the farmhouse dates to 1728. It and the 165-acre farm were bought by the Littles in 1937. They restored the house and, over a period of sixty years, amassed a significant collection of Early American decorative objects: furniture, paintings, decoys, weathervanes, hooked rugs, pottery, and many other objects. In 1984 the Littles transferred ownership of the farm to the SPNEA (now known as Historic New England). After both died in 1993, the house was opened to the public.

The house interior is as it was when Bertram and Nina Little lived here. Alongside the collection are everyday items familiar to the Littles: a television, a typewriter, and other twentieth-century household objects. The atmosphere is not that of a museum but of a home.

Beauport, The Sleeper-McCann House

75 Eastern Point Boulevard
Gloucester, MA 01930
Phone: 978-283-0800
www.historicnewengland/historic-properties/homes/
Beauport/beauport

Beauport was the creation of Henry Davis Sleeper (1878–1934), a Bostonian, an interior designer, and an antiquarian. Beginning in 1907–1908, he built a modest Arts-and-Crafts–style cottage as a weekend and summer retreat. As time progressed Sleeper added to the house several times. After his death the house and its contents were bought by Helena Woolworth McCann and her husband Charles. Mrs. McCann (1878–1938) was the daughter of F. W. Woolworth, the founder of the department store chain of that name. This came to be known as the Sleeper-McCann House. The McCanns made only slight changes. In 1947 their heirs donated the property to the Society for the Preservation of New England Antiquities (Historic New England).

This charming house has about forty rooms, each focusing on a different theme, historic person, color, or shape. The house is full of Sleeper's magnificent collection of Early American furnishings and decorative arts, and objects from Europe and Asia.

The former gatehouse is the visitor center today, and the gardens overlook Gloucester Harbor, with a fine view of Hammond Castle (see page 89) across the way.

MASTER MARINER'S
ROOM, BEAUPORT
Courtesy of Historic New
England

HAMMOND CASTLE

Courtesy of Hammond Castle

Hammond Castle Museum

80 Hesperus Avenue
Gloucester, MA 01930
Phone: 978-283-2080
www.hammondcastle.org

If you're searching New England for a true castle inspired by the castles of medieval Europe, look no further. Perched on a cliff overlooking scenic Gloucester Harbor, this castle was built by John Hayes Hammond Jr. (1888–1965) as a wedding gift for his wife, Irene Fenton (1880–1959). Hammond was an inventor with four hundred patents to his credit—second in number only to those of Thomas Alva Edison (1847–1931). One of Hammond's inventions earned him the title "Father of Remote Control."

A self-guided tour leads visitors to the Great Hall and its magnificent organ, on which Virgil Fox (1912–1980) and other great artists have performed. The tour continues on to the Renaissance dining room, an inner courtyard with medieval facades, the library, bedrooms, kitchens, servants' living quarters, other rooms, and what was a secret passageway. One room exhibits the life and work of John Hammond. His vast collection of ancient Roman, medieval, and Renaissance art and artifacts is displayed throughout the castle.

1830 Brick Dwelling, Hancock Shaker Village

34 Lebanon Mountain Road

Hancock, MA 01237

Phone: 800-817-1137

www.hancockshakervillage.org

'Tis the gift to be simple

'Tis the gift to be free

'Tis the gift to come down

Where we ought to be

And when we find ourselves

In the place just right,

'Twill be in the valley

Of love and delight.

—ELDER JOSEPH, "SIMPLE GIFTS"

The Shakers began in Manchester, England in 1747 and came to America in 1774. Their tenets were communal living, gender equality, celibacy, and pacifism. The name *Shaker* reflects their exuberance during worship services. The Shaker village in Hancock dates to 1783 and was the third of nineteen Shaker communities started in the States. Other villages were in New York, Maine, Kentucky, Ohio, and Indiana. By the mid-nineteenth century there were about five thousand Shakers, three hundred of whom lived on the three-thousand-acre Hancock farm. Their numbers dwindled in the twentieth century, and the Hancock community closed in 1960. The property was sold for use as a museum.

The 1830 Brick Dwelling is a large red-brick building which had sleeping accommodations for about one hundred people. The brothers and sisters lived in separate areas. A visit to the 1830 Brick Dwelling includes bedrooms, the dining room, the meeting room, and the kitchen, all of which display Shaker furniture (chairs, tables, candle stands and other pieces) and Shaker objects. The village has twenty buildings in which there are twenty-two thousand Shaker artifacts.

1830 BRICK DWELLING

Courtesy of Hancock Shaker Village

Fruitlands Farmhouse and Museum

102 Prospect Hill Road
Harvard, MA 01451
Phone: 978-456-3924
www.fruitlands.org

Fruitlands is a part of the legacy of Amos Bronson Alcott (1799–1888). The father of Louisa May Alcott (1832–1888), Amos was a reformer, a teacher, a writer, and a strong advocate of the philosophical movement known as Transcendentalism. To live these ideals, he and Charles Lane (1800–1870) bought this ninety-acre farm in 1843, naming it Fruitlands for its small orchard. Here Alcott, his family, and others gathered a Utopian community, endeavoring to live self-sufficiently, subsisting only on the crops grown by the labor of their hands. Unfortunately there was a divide between the ideal and the real. The experiment failed, the community disbanded, and in 1845 the Alcott family returned to Concord and lived in the house which in time came to be known as The Wayside (see page 76).

In 1910, Fruitlands was bought by Clara Endicott Sears, who restored the farmhouse and opened it for tours in 1914. In 2016 the 210-acre Fruitlands property was transferred to the care of The Trustees of Reservations, the oldest regional land trust in the world. Formed in 1891, The Trustees oversee 116 properties and 27,000 acres throughout the Commonwealth of Massachusetts.

The farmhouse looks as it did when the Alcotts were in residence, and it has exhibits regarding the family and Transcendentalism. In addition, there are three gallery buildings on the property: the Shaker Museum, which is housed in a building moved here from Hancock Shaker Village, (see page 90); the Native American Museum; and the Art Museum, which exhibits American art, most notably that of the Hudson River School. Special exhibits are periodically mounted. The 210-acre museum property overlooking the Nashoba Valley has walking trails to explore.

The Great House on Castle Hill

The Crane Estate

290 Argilla Road

Ipswich, MA 01938

Phone: 978-356-4351

www.thetrustees.org/places-to-visit/north-shore
/castle-hill-crane.html

O f all the houses in this book, this may be the one with the most dramatic setting. This is a 2,100-acre estate. The Great House sits atop a 165-acre drumlin and is surrounded by a vast expanse of gardens, salt marshes, beaches, a bay, and the Atlantic Ocean.

The story of this magnificent property begins in 1637, when it was deeded to John Winthrop (1606–1676), the founder of Ipswich. The land went through several owners before it was bought in 1910 by Richard Teller Crane (1873–1931). He was based in Chicago and was heir to and president of the Crane Company, which manufactured plumbing fixtures. On top of the hill, he built an Italian Renaissance–style villa with stucco walls and a red-tile roof. His wife Florence (1893–1949) disliked the house. Mr. Crane asked her to live within it for ten years. He promised her that if she still didn't like it at the end of the trial period, he would have the villa demolished and build another house on its site to her liking. She agreed.

Ten years passed and she got her wish. In 1924 the villa was demolished, and the seventeenth-century Jacobean-style house that replaced it was completed four years later. The architect was David Adler (1882–1949) of Chicago. The interior is fitted with wood paneling from English homes, including carvings in the library by the eighteenth-century English master Grinling Gibbons (1648–1721).

The landscape architects were the Olmsted Brothers (see page 64). Extending out from the terrace at the back of the house is a Grand Allée (160 feet wide and half a mile long), which slopes down the hill to the water. It is flanked by trees and marble statues. The property includes a casino with a saltwater pool and twenty-one outbuildings.

Mr. Crane died in 1931, and Mrs. Crane followed him in 1949. She willed the estate to The Trustees of Reservations.

The Mount

2 Plunkett Street
Lenox, MA 01240
Phone: 413-551-5111
www.edithwharton.org

"On a slope over-looking the dark waters and densely-wooded shore
of Laurel Lake we built a spacious and dignified house, to which we
gave the name of my great-grandfather's place, the Mount ... there
for ten years I lived and gardened and wrote contentedly ..."

—EDITH WHARTON

Edith Wharton (1862–1937) was the Pulitzer Prize–winning author of fifteen novels, seven novellas, eighty-five short stories, poems, books on subjects as diverse as travel and design, and a memoir. Some of her best known works are *The Age of Innocence, The House of Mirth, Ethan Frome,* and *The Buccaneers.* In 1897 she and Ogden Codman Jr. (1863–1951) coauthored *The Decoration of Houses.* Most Victorian house interiors were dark, cluttered, and heavily draped. Wharton and Codman instead advocated eighteenth-century French design: less clutter and more light.

Edith designed her house in 1902 with the help of Codman and Francis L. V. Hoppin (1867–1941). The model for the exterior was the seventeenth-century Belton House in England. The interior, however, is a blend of Italian, English, and French prototypes.

Mounted on a fieldstone foundation and terrace, the mansion stands three stories tall and is white stucco, its windows framed by green shutters. The roof is pierced with dormers and tall white chimneys, and it is topped by a cupola surrounded by a balustrade.

Edith and her husband Edward Wharton lived here until 1911. The building was sold and remained a residence for a while. It then became a school dormitory and later a performance space for the theatrical company Shakespeare & Co. In 1976 The Mount was bought by Edith Wharton Restoration.

The property originally consisted of 128 acres and now has 49.5. There are restored gardens to explore and enjoy: an Alpine rock garden, an Italian walled garden, a formal flower garden, grass terraces, a lime walk, and

trails through the surrounding woods. The grounds also contain a greenhouse and a Georgian Revival gatehouse and stable.

Special note: Another house museum in Lenox is Ventfort Hall and
Gilded Age Museum. It was built in 1893 for Sarah Morgan, the sister of J. P.
Morgan. For information visit http://gildedage.org/.

Frelinghuysen Morris House and Studio

92 Hawthorne Street
Lenox, MA 01240
Phone: 413-637-0166
www.frelinghuysen.org

This was the home of a married couple, each an abstract artist with works in the collection of the Metropolitan Museum of Art, and each with a fascinating life history.

George L. K. Morris (1905–1975) was from a prominent New York City family. He was a descendant of Lewis Morris (1726–1798), a signer of the Declaration of Independence. As such, he was kin to Aletta Morris, whose Newport home Chepstow is also featured in this book (see page 167). After graduating from Groton and Yale, George pursued a career as a writer, editor, and abstract artist. In 1930 he built a studio on Brookhurst, his parents' Lenox summer estate, and then he added his house in 1941. The architect was John Butler Swann, and the style used was evocative of the German Bauhaus school.

In 1935 George married Suzy Frelinghuysen (1911–1988). She was originally from New Jersey and, like her husband, was from a prosperous family. Suzy had a successful career as a soprano singing for the New York City Opera. After a bout of bronchitis in 1951, Frelinghuysen retired from singing, turning her talents to abstract painting. In her will Suzy directed that the house be opened to the public as a museum.

The property covers forty-six acres; the house stands two stories high and is glass-block and stucco. It contains not only frescoes, sculptures, and paintings by Suzy and by George, but also their collection of American and European Cubist art. Among these are works by Pablo Picasso, Henri Matisse, Joan Miro, and Georges Braque.

Hancock-Clarke House

36 Hancock Street
Lexington, MA 02420
Phone: 781-861-0928
www.lexingtonhistory.org

"There, I guess King George will be able to read that without his
spectacles!"

—JOHN HANCOCK, AFTER SIGNING THE DECLARATION OF
INDEPENDENCE

John Hancock (1736/7–1793), governor, president of the Second Continental Congress, and patriot, was the first to sign the Declaration of Independence. His large, stylized signature on that document has become synonymous with signatures in general (e.g., "Put your John Hancock here"). Significantly, this is the only house standing today in which he lived.

The story begins in 1699. John's grandfather, the Reverend John Hancock (1671–1752), bought this property and in 1738 built this two-story wood-frame parsonage. When his son died in 1744, the Reverend Hancock's seven-year-old grandson John (later known as The Signer) came to live here for six years until he was adopted by his uncle.

In 1752 the parsonage passed to the Reverend Jonas Clarke (1730–1805), who lived here with his wife and their twelve children.

Fast forward to April 18 and 19, 1775. Both Samuel Adams (1722–1803) and John Hancock were overnight guests here. They had just attended the Massachusetts Provincial Congress in Concord and were fearful that they might be captured by the British en route back to Boston. That night Paul Revere and John Dawes made their famous midnight ride to Lexington and Concord to warn that British troops were coming. Once warned, Hancock and Adams were spirited on to Burlington, Massachusetts.

The parsonage remained in the Clarke family until 1844. The Lexington Historical Society acquired the house in 1896. It has furnishings and portraits that were owned by the Hancocks and the Clarkes, as well as artifacts and relics of that famous night in April 1776. The Historical Society also maintains other properties in town closely associated with the American Revolution.

GROPIUS HOUSE

Courtesy of Historic New

England

Gropius House

68 Baker Bridge Road
Lincoln, MA 01773
Phone: 781-259-8098
www.historicnewengland/homes/GropiusHouse/gropius-house

"We want to create the purely organic building, boldly emanating its inner laws, free of untruths or ornamentation."

—WALTER GROPIUS

Walter Gropius (1883–1969) was a German architect and for some years a founding director of the German school known as the Bauhaus. In 1937 he accepted a post on the faculty of Harvard's Graduate School of Design, and the following year he applied his design principles when he built this house for himself and his wife Ise.

The list of guests who stayed here is a virtual who's who of twentieth-century contemporary design: Frank Lloyd Wright, Alexander Calder, Henry Moore, Marcel Breuer, and more. Walter died in 1969, and Ise passed in 1983. The house and its contents were bequeathed to Historic New England.

Though many of the building materials (wood, brick, and fieldstone) are those common to New England buildings, the house in many ways departs from tradition. It is a simple design, and it has a flat roof and an interior with an open floor plan.

The Gropius House contains art by Henry Moore, Joan Miro, and others, and the furniture is the work of Marcel Breuer, Eero Saarinen, and Yori Yanagi, all masters of modern art and design.

Nearby, also in the town of Lincoln, there is another property of Historic New England, Codman Estate, which dates to about 1740 (www.historicnewengland.com).

Jeremiah Lee Mansion

151 Washington Street
Marblehead, MA 01945
Phone: 781-631-1768
www.marbleheadmuseum.org/properties/lee-mansion

Fishermen from Cornwall, England, and the English Channel Islands came to this rocky peninsula in 1629. In colonial times Marblehead was a major port and a shipbuilding center.

The wealthiest ship owner and merchant in colonial Massachusetts was Colonel Jeremiah Lee (c.1721–1791). This stately house was built for him in 1768. The house is wood, though the facade appears to be stone. Sand was thrown on the freshly painted exterior, creating the illusion of a stone surface. The house is nine bays across, rises three stories, and is topped with a cupola or belvedere from which there are expansive views.

The grand entrance hall has a wide staircase paneled with mahogany. On either side hang portraits of Jeremiah and Martha Lee by the renowned Boston artist John Singleton Copley (1738–1815). The interior is embellished with finely carved woodwork in the Rococo style, and with original hand-painted eighteenth-century English wallpaper depicting idealized ancient Roman ruins. Much of the period furniture is the work of Marblehead, Salem, and Boston cabinetmakers. Eighteenth- and nineteenth-century decorative items include ceramics, silver, clocks, and textiles.

The property includes a garden. It and the mansion have been owned and maintained by the Marblehead Museum and Historical Society since 1909.

The Royall House and Slave Quarters

15 George Street
Medford, MA 02155
Phone: 781-396-9032
www.royallhouse.org

This historic site is an eye-opener for many. It has the oldest surviving separate slave living quarters in the northern United States, a reminder that slavery existed in Massachusetts until it was outlawed in 1783.

Isaac Royall Sr. (1677–1739) was from New England, and he made his fortune in Antigua as the owner of a sugar plantation. In 1732, after deciding to return to Massachusetts, he bought a modest farmhouse and more than five hundred acres near Boston. Royall had the house enlarged and transformed into the spacious and beautiful three-story Georgian manor house we see today. He named his country estate Ten Hill Farm. Royall had a brick Out Kitchen built just a few feet from his house. He brought twenty-seven of his slaves with him from his sugar plantation. Some lived in the upper story of the Out Kitchen. The Out Kitchen was expanded in 1760 with a clapboard addition that provided housing for more slaves. Some of them worked inside as domestic servants; others worked on the farm in the production of cider, the manufacture of wool, and the harvesting of grass for hay.

When Royall died in 1739 his estate was inherited by his son Isaac Royall Jr. (1719–1781). The younger Royall was a Loyalist. During the American Revolution he moved to Canada and ultimately to England. His estate was taken by the Patriots and later used by Generals Washington, Lee, Stark, and Sullivan. It is said that George Washington interrogated two British soldiers in the Marble Chamber.

In 1804 the house returned to a member of the Royall family. It then had a number of owners and succumbed to the effects of time and neglect.

In 1898, recognizing the historic significance and beauty of the house, the Daughters of the American Revolution mounted a loan exhibition of colonial furniture and artifacts. In 1907 the Royall House Association was begun, and the following year the house, slave quarters, and a small parcel of land were bought and the museum was later opened. Restoration of the property, including the slave quarters, is ongoing.

THE ROYALL
HOUSE AND SLAVE
QUARTERS
Lee Snider Photo Images /
Shutterstock.com

Forbes House Museum

215 Adams Street
Milton, MA 02186
Phone: 617-696-1815
www.forbeshousemuseum.org

The Forbes House Museum is notable for several reasons: its site, its history, its architecture, and its collections. On top of Milton Hill, the house has views of Boston Harbor and the city's skyline in the distance. This is a Greek Revival building which, interestingly, incorporates some nautical features like an elliptical staircase similar to those often found in lighthouses. In 1833 it was commissioned by two brothers: one was the captain, ship owner, and China Trade merchant Robert Bennet Forbes (1804–1889), and the other was John Murray Forbes (1813–1898), a railroad magnate, merchant, abolitionist, and philanthropist. Together they gifted the house to their mother, Margaret Perkins (1773–1856). Four generations of the Forbes family lived here until the 1960s, when it became a museum.

The collections here are vast and varied. The China Trade collection includes nineteenth-century export porcelain, paintings, portraits, and furniture. Other artifacts include European and American art, silver, and decorative objects. The last family member to live here was Mary Bowditch Forbes (1878–1962), who had a particular interest in the American Civil War and Abraham Lincoln. She gathered a collection of memorabilia relating to both and, in 1923, built on this property a replica of the Kentucky cabin Lincoln was born in. A tour of the house includes the kitchen and a glimpse into the lives of the Irish immigrant servants who worked here.

Special note: Also in Milton, near the Forbes House Museum, is the Eustis Estate Museum and Study Center. Built in 1878, the stone and brick house covers 18,600 square feet and stands on eighty acres. It was opened to the public by Historic New England (www.historicnewengland.org) in 2017.

The Oldest House

16 Sunset Hill
Nantucket, MA 02554
Phone: 508-228-1894
https://www.nha.org/sites/oldesthouse.html

> *"Two thirds of this terraqueous globe are the Nantucketer's.*
> *For the sea is his, he owns it, as Emperors own empires."*
>
> —HERMAN MELVILLE, *MOBY-DICK*

Nantucket, thirty miles south of Cape Cod, is an idyllic island just fifteen miles long and six miles wide. Its name originated with the Wampanoag people, who spoke the Algonquin language. Its translation is unclear, but the most popular one is "far away island." The first European to set foot on Nantucket was an Englishman, Bartholomew Gosnold, in 1602. The island was deeded to Thomas Mayhew, who in 1659 sold it to the Nine Original Purchasers "for the sum of thirty pounds . . . and also two beaver hats, one for myself, and one for my wife." The island became a haven for Quakers. Fishing, trading, and shipbuilding were the Quakers' first industries. In the eighteenth century, whaling was the biggest business here, and "The Little Gray Lady of the Sea" was home port to more than 125 whaling ships. (Two characters in Melville's *Moby-Dick*, Ahab and Starbuck, were from Nantucket.) By the 1850s the whaling industry had waned here and grown in New Bedford because of the latter's access to the railroad, which was used in the transport of whale oil (see the Rotch-Jones-Duff House on page 107).

One of the Nine Original Purchasers was Tristam Coffin. In 1686 this house was built as a wedding gift for Jethro Coffin—Tristam's grandson—and his bride Mary Gardner. The Jethro Coffin House, as this is also known, is the oldest house on Nantucket Island and the only building still in existence from the Nantucket's original seventeenth-century settlement. Jethro sold his house to Nathaniel Paddock in 1708, and by the 1840s it was the property of a cooper, George Turner. The Turner family abandoned the house in the 1860s. Things began to change for the better with the Coffin family reunion in 1881. The gathering sparked a renewed interest in the house, its history, and its maintenance. The

Nantucket Historical Association bought it in 1923, restored it, and opened it to the public. The house was further restored with the expertise of John Milner Architects, Inc. after it was struck by lightning in 1987. An eighteenth-century-style herb and vegetable kitchen garden was added in 2006, and an apple orchard was planted.

This is a one-and-a-half-story saltbox house, the saltbox design being created when a lean-to was added in the early part of the eighteenth century. From outside, the large red-brick central chimney may be seen, on which there is a design in brick best described as an inverted letter "U." This has been the topic of much conjecture. Some think it depicts a horseshoe, and so this is also sometimes referred to as "The Horseshoe House." Others say it is simply a seventeenth-century English (or Jacobean) decorative motif. And still others think it is a hex to ward off witches of the Salem Witch Trials variety.

The Nantucket Historical Association also owns and maintains other historic properties that are open to visitors, including the Whaling Museum (housed in an 1846 candle factory), the Fire Hose Cart House (1886), the Old Mill (1746), the Quaker Meeting House (1845), the Old Gaol (1806), the 1800 House, the Hadwin House (1845), and Greater Light, a late-eighteenth-century livestock barn that later became a summer home and art studio.

The Cushing House

98 High Street
Newburyport, MA 01950
Phone: 978-462-2681
www.newburyhistory.org

The English settled Newbury in 1635, and in 1764 the port became a separate town. Ideally situated at the mouth of the Merrimack River, Newburyport thrived in colonial times and became a major shipbuilding center. Following the Revolution, shipbuilding continued, reaching its height in the 1840s when Newburyport's shipyards produced clipper ships.

Built in 1808, this twenty-room house eventually became the home of Caleb Cushing (1800–1879), who had a long career in public service, first as the United States minister to Spain and then as minister to China, US congressman, and attorney general under President Franklin Pierce. The house remained in his family until 1955, when it was given to the Historical Society of Old Newbury. The red-brick house, forty feet long on all sides, is an excellent example of a Federal-style house. Its interior has the atmosphere of an affluent New England ship-owner's home and is a treasure trove of period furnishings, portraits, maritime memorabilia, a clock collection, and objects collected on overseas voyages. Outside one can find the cobblestone yard, carriage house, fruit trees, and nineteenth-century flower garden.

Rotch-Jones-Duff House and Gardens Museum

396 County Street
New Bedford, MA 02740
Phone: 508-997-1401
http://rjdmuseum.org

"Nowhere in all America will you find more patrician-like houses;

parks and gardens more opulent, than in New Bedford... all these

brave houses and flowery gardens..."

—HERMAN MELVILLE , *MOBY-DICK*

This area was settled by colonists from Plymouth in 1652 and for many years was a part of the town of Dartmouth. "New" Bedford was established in 1787, its name distinguishing it from Bedford, Massachusetts. As early as the 1760s, this was a whaling and shipbuilding center. By the 1820s New Bedford was one of the largest and busiest whaling ports in the world and home to ten thousand seamen. Herman Melville was one of them, and was inspired to pen his classic *Moby-Dick* here. While the whaling industry is but a memory, New Bedford's economy is still very much tied to the sea, as it is the East Coast's largest fishing port.

This historic property is named for three owner-families. Each was a leader in New Bedford's whaling industry, and each made a significant contribution to this house and its gardens.

The first owner was William Rotch Jr. (1759–1850), who was not only a wealthy whaler but also a philanthropist. Though this one-block, one-acre site was in a neighborhood of mansions, Rotch wanted his house to be relatively modest. The architect chosen was Richard Upjohn (1802–1878). The year was 1834, and Upjohn had migrated to New Bedford from Britain just five years earlier. Richard Upjohn would later move on to New York City, becoming the first President of the American Institute of Architects and a champion of Gothic Revival architecture. His best known work is Trinity Church, Wall Street, New York City. Another of his works is Kingscote in Newport (see page 174).

After Rotch died in 1850 the house was bought by Edward Coffin Jones (1805–1880), a Nantucket ship owner. During his ownership the pergola

was added to the garden. His daughter, Amelia Hickling Jones (1849–1935), lived here for eighty-five years. When she died she left no heirs.

The following year, 1936, the property was bought by Mark Duff (1891–1967), a descendant of a whaling family. Duff enchanced the garden with ornamental ponds, walkways, and seven thousand tulips. In 1981 his descendants sold the house and its gardens to the Waterfront Historic Area League (WHALE), which has been a major force in establishing the New Bedford Historic District, a National Historic Landmark. The Rotch-Jones-Duff House was first opened for tours in 1983.

The house is a masterpiece of the Greek Revival style, and its furnishings, decor, and collection are original. The garden has a parterre rose garden with tall calla lilies, a cutting garden, and a "woodland walk" surrounding a nineteenth-century wooden latticework pergola.

Other sites of the New Bedford Whaling National Historic Park (www.nps.gov/nebe/index.htm) are nearby.

Herman Melville's Arrowhead

780 Holmes Road
Pittsfield, MA 01201
Phone: 413-442-1793
http://mobydick.org/

*"On the higher side of Pittsfield, sits Herman Melville, shaping out
the gigantic conception of his 'white whale' while the giant shape of
[Mount] Graylock looms upon him from his study window."*

—NATHANIEL HAWTHORNE

The scene Hawthorne describes would have taken place around 1850. Herman Melville (1819–1891) had just moved here with his wife Lizzie and their son Malcolm. They would live in this farmhouse for the next thirteen years. Here Melville wrote not only *Moby-Dick* but also his novels *Pierre, The Confidence-Man, Israel Potter*, and his collection of short stories *The Piazza Tales* ("piazza" referring to Arrowhead's porch).

At first a country inn, Arrowhead had been built for Captain David Bush in the 1780s. The wood-frame, clapboard house was sold to Dr. John Brewer in 1844.

Melville was no stranger to the area. He often visited his Uncle Thomas, who owned the abutting property, and Herman seized the opportunity to buy Arrowhead in 1850. Farming and writing here, Melville was not able to make ends meet. In 1863 Herman and his brother Allan (1823–1872) traded their houses through sale, and Herman moved to Allan's former house at 104 East Twenty-Sixth Street in Manhattan. There Herman earned his living as a customs officer, a profession he shared, by coincidence, with his friend Nathaniel Hawthorne.

Arrowhead stayed in the family until 1927. There were other owners, and then in 1975 the Berkshire County Historical Society acquired the property, restored the house, and opened it to the public.

Jabez Howland House

33 Sandwich Street
Plymouth, MA 02360
Phone: 508-746-9590
www.pilgrimjohnhowlandsociety.org

What do Humphrey Bogart, Ralph Waldo Emerson, George H. W. Bush, Alec Baldwin, Franklin Delano Roosevelt, Lillian Russell, Sarah Palin, Henry Wadsworth Longfellow, and Dr. Benjamin Spock all have in common? They are all descendants of Mayflower Pilgrim John Howland (c. 1591–1672/3). And John Howland almost didn't make it to America. On the voyage here he fell overboard. Luckily he grabbed onto a rope and was hauled on board.

At first an indentured servant, Howland later became the secretary and assistant to Governor John Carver (before 1584–1621). Howland signed the Mayflower Compact and helped found Plimouth Colony.

This house belonged not to John but to his son Jabez (c. 1644–before 1712). It had been built in 1667 for Jacob Mitchell. When his father's house burned, Jabez invited his parents to live here. And so this is the only surviving house in Plymouth in which a Pilgrim lived. Jabez sold the house in 1680 when he moved to Rhode Island. It remained a private residence until 1915, was restored, and is now owned and operated by the Pilgrim John Howland Society. The house is filled with period furniture and artifacts, much of which belonged to the Howlands. Tours are given by very gracious and knowledgeable guides dressed in period costume.

Dwellings of Plimoth Plantation

137 Warren Avenue
Plymouth, MA 02360
Phone: 508-746-1622
www.plimoth.org

"[Plimoth]is well situated upon a high hill close to the seaside. . . . In this
plantation is about twenty houses, four or five of which are very fair and
peasant, and the rest (as time will serve) shall be made better. And this
town is in such manner that it makes a great street between the houses . . .
and lastly, the town is furnished with a company of honest men . . ."

—EMMANUEL ALTHAM, A VISITOR IN 1623

Before the coming of the English, this area was called Patuxet by the Wampanoag people. It was visited twice by Europeans before the arrival of the Pilgrims, first in 1605 by Samuel de Champlain (1574–1635), who called this Port St. Louis. Then Captain John Smith (1580–1631) named it "New Plimoth" after an English city in 1614. Captain Smith's place names seemed to stick, as he also dubbed the wider region "New England."

The Pilgrims (both Puritans and Strangers) arrived here on December 12, 1620. Many did not survive the first winter, with little shelter and almost no food. The Wampanoag neighbors gave food to the Pilgrims and showed them how to grow corn and other crops. After the first harvest in 1621, both the English and the Indians joined in what has traditionally been called the first Thanksgiving.

Plimoth Plantation as we know it today was begun by Henry Hornblower II (1917–1985). A Bostonian and a financial analyst, his love for Plymouth and its history began when he was a boy spending summers on his family's Plymouth estate. In 1947 Hornblower built two English cottages, and ten years later the Mayflower II sailed from England to America and permanently docked here. The reproduction English Village was built on its present site in 1959, and the Wampanoag Homesite was built in 1973.

Frozen in time, the small English maritime and farming village appears today as it was in the 1620s. The houses that populate the Plantation today are as described by the visitor Altham. Cottages are modest in size, have dirt floors and thatched roofs, and are sparely furnished with reproductions of seventeenth-century English furniture. Kitchen gardens complete the plots. This is a living history museum, and the guide-interpreters in the village are not just dressed in period costume. They also play the roles of specific Pilgrims and speak with the vocabulary and accent of seventeenth-century English folk. Don't confuse them with conversation about cars or cell phones. They won't know what you're talking about!

The Wampanoag Homesite is located along the shore of the Eel River. Clustered here are "wigwams" or houses. The "wetu" is a mat-covered house. The "nush wetu" is a long house covered with bark, and within there are three firepits. Guide-interpreters are Native Americans dressed in historically correct attire, most of which is deerskin. The guides speak in modern American English and engage visitors in conversations about the Native people who lived here in the seventeenth century, along with their lives, work, and activities, including fishing, hunting, and the growing of crops.

In addition to the homesite and village, Plimoth Plantation has the Hornblower Visitor Center, Craft Center, Maxwell and Nye Barns, and the Gristmill. The *Mayflower II*, an accurate re-creation of the Pilgrims' ship, is docked in downtown Plymouth and welcomes visitors on board.

Houses of Adams National Historical Park

1250 Hancock Street
Quincy, MA 02169
Phone: 617-770-1175
https://www.nps.gov/adam/index.htm

The Adams National Historical Park includes eleven buildings connected with five generations of the Adams family for more than two centuries, from 1720 to 1927. Of those sites, three were homes of the Adams family. Visits to each begin at the park's visitor center at 1250 Hancock Street.

John Adams Birthplace

The John Adams birthplace was built on what was known as the "Old Coast Road" in colonial times. This saltbox house was constructed in 1681 for Joseph Penniman. The elder John Adams (1692–1761), church deacon, lieutenant, and town selectman, bought it in 1720. His son John Adams (1735–1826), contributing author of the Declaration of Independence, America's first vice president and second president, was born here in 1735. When the elder John died in 1761, it was inherited by his son Peter Boylston Adams, and he in turn sold it to his brother John in 1774. It remained in the family until 1940, when it was sold to the City of Quincy and became a site of the Quincy Historical Society. Today it belongs to the National Park Service.

John Quincy Adams Birthplace

The birthplace of John Quincy Adams (1767–1848) is another two-and-a-half-story wood-frame saltbox house, not unlike the birthplace of his father. It was built in 1663 and bought by Deacon John Adams, who in turn gave it to John and Abigail Adams (1744–1818) after their wedding in 1764. Adams had a remarkable political career. One of America's greatest diplomats, he crafted the Treaty of Ghent ending the War of 1812, the Monroe Doctrine, and the Florida Treaty, which led to the annexation of Florida. America's sixth president, he also served as a congressman, senator, secretary of state, and US minister to Russia and to the Court of St. James. Following his term as president, Adams appeared before the US Supreme Court, pleading for, and winning, the freedom of Africans kidnapped and brought to the United States aboard the ship *La Amistad*. The story is retold in the 1997 film *Amistad*. Both presidents and their wives are interred in the crypt of the United First Parish Church, another site in the Adams National Historical Park.

Peacefield

In the Adams family, Peacefield was also known as Old House. This was the home and farm of John Adams, his son John Quincy Adams, and his son Charles Francis Adams (1807–1886). At first a smaller home, it was built for Jamaica sugar planter Leonard Vassall in 1731. While in London, John Adams bought the house and its forty acres sight unseen. On their return they were disappointed with their purchase: low ceilings, two rooms on the first floor, two on the second, plus an attic. Abigail Adams complained, "It feels like a wren's nest." She set about enlarging and embellishing the house, transforming it into a proper Georgian mansion

BIRTHPLACES OF JOHN
AND JOHN QUINCY
ADAMS PAINTED BY
G. FRANKENSTEIN, 1849
Courtesy of National Park Service,
Adams National Historical Park

with a hallway and larger rooms, including a parlor and a study. When her son Charles Francis inherited the house, he added to it as well. The family continued to live here until 1946 when they donated it to the United States.

Not to be missed on the property is the Stone Library. This Gothic Revival building dates to 1870 and houses fourteen thousand books, papers of the two presidents and their descendants, and such significant documents as a copy of George Washington's farewell address. And there is the Mendi Bible given to John Quincy Adams by the Mendi men of the schooner *La Amistad*.

The estate has a formal eighteenth-century flower garden and an apple orchard.

Special note: There are two more historic house museums in Quincy which are not a part of the Adams National Historical Park. One is the Josiah Quincy House, which dates to 1770 (www.historicnewengland .org), and the other is the Dorothy Quincy Homestead, which was built in 1686 (http://nscdama.org/).

Phillips House

34 Chestnut Street
Salem, MA 01970
Phone: 978-744-0440
http://www.historicnewengland.org/historic-properties/
homes/phillips-house

While the historic district around Chestnut Street contains more than four hundred historic buildings, the Phillips House is the only one open for touring.

The house has a long and fascinating history. Oddly, it began not here but rather four miles away in Danvers. In 1819, Captain Nathaniel West inherited one third of a grand house there. He removed his third—which comprised four rooms—and had it brought to this site on logs pulled by oxen. Once here, the captain added a third story, a hall, and an ell kitchen wing in the rear.

The West family lived here until 1836. It then became a "genteel boarding house and school," and then a home again. Through the years the house grew in size, and stylistically it was transformed from a comely Federal design to one more suited to Victorian tastes. Finally, in 1911, Anna Wheatland Phillips bought the house and lived here with her husband Stephen Willard Phillips and their young son, also named Stephen. Over the course of more than a year, the house was updated with modern conveniences such as electricity and indoor plumbing. Stairs were removed, rooms enlarged, and closets added. And the house interior's style was transformed once again, this time into Colonial Revival.

The younger Stephen Phillips died in 1971. He had expressed his wishes that the home he knew as a boy be opened to the public as a museum. His widow formed the Stephen Phillips Memorial Charitable Trust for Historic Preservation to facilitate this, and in 2006 Phillips House became a property of Historic New England.

The house has family furniture, art, oriental rugs, Chinese export porcelain, souvenirs from travels to exotic locations like Polynesia and

Hawaii, personal objects, and memorabilia collected over a span of five generations. The tour includes a look at the servants' living and work areas. A visit is not complete without a glimpse of the carriage house, where vintage cars, century-old carriages, a sleigh, and a buggy are on display.

PHILLIPS HOUSE

Courtesy of Historic New England

Houses of Peabody Essex Museum

East India Square
161 Essex Street
Salem, MA 01970
Phone: 978-745-9500, 866-745-1876
www.pem.org

The Peabody Essex Museum has its roots in two of the oldest museums in the nation: the East India Marine Society (founded in 1799), which later became the Peabody Museum of Salem, and the Essex Institute, founded in 1848. The museums combined as one in 1992, and the PEM has grown to a collection of 1.3 million objects and twenty-two historic buildings. Five of these are historic houses reviewed in this chapter.

Chinese House Yin Yu Tang

Yin Yu Tang is translated as "Hall of Plentiful Shelter." This house was built for a wealthy merchant around 1800, and for two hundred years and through eight generations it was home to the Huang family in the village of Huang Cun in the mountainous Anhui province of China. Successive generations of male descendants, their wives, and their children lived in the house. As many as three generations of the family lived here at a given time, with up to twenty or thirty people in the sixteen-bedroom house. The last family members lived in the house in 1980. Through partnership with Chinese officials in the Huizhou region, the house was meticulously dismantled, shipped to America, reassembled on this site, and opened to the public in 2003. Yin Yu Tang is the only intact antique Chinese house outside of China.

Approaching Yin Yu Tang, visitors pass through a forecourt. The house has a timber frame, masonry walls of brick and sandstone, and a tile roof. Once inside, there is a two-story central court—or "sky well"—with fish ponds. The self-guided tour covers two floors with reception halls, bedrooms, and a kitchen. The house is embellished with brick carvings, wallpaper, lattice windows, masonry paintings, furniture, and household objects.

John Ward House

This house was built on Prison Lane (now St. Peter Street) around 1684 and stood opposite the prison during the Salem witch trials. This is a First Period home with many post-medieval features: steeply-pitched gables, a second-story overhang, a batten door, an asymmetrical facade, diamond-paned leaded casement windows, and a large central chimney.

The house was moved three blocks to this site in 1910. It was split in two, put on rolling logs, and pulled by oxen. Preservationist and museum curator George Francis Dow (1868–1936) led the restoration effort.

Crowningshield-Bentley House

When built in 1724, this was a half house. It was enlarged with additions in 1761 and again in 1794. It was home to ship captain John Crowningshield (1696–1761). A boarder in the house was the Reverend William Bentley (1759–1819), a well known Unitarian minister, writer, and journalist. His library was the second largest in the nation after that of Thomas Jefferson.

Gardner-Pingree House

John Gardner was a Salem merchant. In 1804 he commissioned Samuel McIntire (1757–1811) to design this house, which is one of McIntire's finest and best preserved works. In 1834 David Pingree became the owner. A century later his descendants donated the house to the Essex Institute.

This house has the dubious distinction of being the site of a well-known murder. On the night of April 6, 1830, Captain Joseph White was killed in his sleep. The prosecutor at the murderer's trial was Daniel Webster (1782–1852). Edgar Allan Poe wrote the short story "The Tell-Tale Heart" based on the murder, and Nathaniel Hawthorne's *The Scarlet Letter* was inspired in part by the crime.

Ropes Mansion and Garden

This fifteen-room Georgian mansion was built around 1727 and was lived in by four generations of the Ropes family. The house was restored by the PEM and reopened to the public in 2015. It has many original furnishings: eighteenth- and nineteenth-century furniture, decorative objects, kitchen items, and personal items.

Nathaniel Hawthorne's Birthplace

115 Derby Street
Salem, MA 01970
Phone: 978-744-0991
www.7gables.org/about/history/
nathaniel-hawthorne-birthplace/

> *"I was born in the town of Salem, Massachusetts, in a house built by*
> *my grandfather, who was a maritime personage. The old household*
> *estate was in another part of town, and had descended in the family*
> *ever since the settlement of the country; but this old man of the*
> *sea exchanged it for a lot of land situated near the wharves, and*
> *convenient to his business, where he built the house . . . and laid out*
> *a garden, where I rolled on a grass-plot under an apple-tree and*
> *picked abundant currants."*
>
> —NATHANIEL HAWTHORNE

The house Hawthorne (1804–1864) refers to was originally at 27 Union Street in Salem and moved to this site in 1958. Boston mariner Joshua Pickman built it around 1750. There is evidence that some of the timbers in the house may be from a seventeenth-century house that had stood on the same site. In 1765 Nathaniel's grandfather Daniel Hathorne (the "w" was later added to the surname) moved into this house with his wife, Rachel Phelps, and their children. Nathaniel's parents moved into the house in 1801, and he was born here in 1804. His older sister Elizabeth recounts that Nathaniel was born "in the chamber over that little parlor . . . in that house on Union Street. It then belonged to my grandmother Hawthorne, who lived in one part of it. There we lived until 1808, when my father died, at Surinam."

In 1842 Hawthorne married Sophia Peabody (1809–1871). They made their home successively in several places, including two residences in Concord, Massachusetts: The Old Manse (see page 75) and The Wayside (see page 76). A prolific writer, Nathaniel penned many novels, short stories, and short story collections. His best-known and most-loved works include *The House of the Seven Gables (1851), The Scarlet Letter (1850),* and *Twice-Told Tales* (1837).

This red clapboard Georgian house has Hawthorne family furniture, memorabilia, and displays about the author, his life, and his work.

Special note: Nathaniel Hawthorne's Birthplace is accessible through the visitor center of The House of the Seven Gables.

The House of the Seven Gables

115 Derby Street
Salem, MA 01970
Phone: 978-744-0991
www.7gables.org

> *"Halfway down a by-street of one of our New England towns stands*
> *a rusty wooded house, with seven acutely peaked gables, facing*
> *towards various points of the compass, and a huge, clustered*
> *chimney in the midst . . . the aspect of the venerable mansion has*
> *always affected me like a human countenance, bearing the traces*
> *not merely of outward storm and sunshine, but expressive also, of*
> *the long lapse of mortal life, and accompanying vicissitudes that*
> *have passed within."*
>
> —NATHANIEL HAWTHORNE, *THE HOUSE OF THE SEVEN GABLES*

The House of the Seven Gables, also known as the Turner-Ingersoll House Mansion, is one of the oldest timber-frame houses in the nation. It was built in 1668 for a wealthy merchant, John Turner. It remained in his family for three generations, spanning more than a century. At first a modest two-and-a-half-story house, over the years it was enlarged into a fourteen-room mansion. It was also transformed into a Georgian design, and in the process some of the gables were removed.

In 1782 the house was sold to another wealthy merchant, Captain Samuel Ingersoll. The Ingersolls were cousins to Nathaniel Hawthorne. While Hawthorne lived and worked in Salem as a customs officer at the nearby Customs House, he would sometimes visit the captain's daughter Susanna. She related to him the history of the house, took him to the attic, and showed him where some of the gables had been. Hawthorne was thus inspired to write *The House of the Seven Gables* in 1851. Susanna died in 1858, and in 1879 her adopted son Horace Connolly sold the house to absentee landlords.

The next owners were Henry and Elizabeth Upton. After buying the house in 1883 they opened it as a museum, charging a nominal fee. And then in 1908, philanthropist and preservationist Caroline Emmerton bought the house. She had it restored by architect Joseph Chandler, who had also restored the Paul Revere House (see page 60). The house became not only a museum but also the site of The House of the Seven Gables Settlement Association, which helped and educated the Polish and Russian immigrant population in the neighborhood. The income realized from the admission fees helped finance the efforts of the settlement house.

Since the House of the Seven Gables became a museum, five historic houses from the seventeenth, eighteenth, and nineteenth centuries have been moved to this campus, which is now a national historic district. These are the Nathaniel Hawthorne Birthplace (c. 1750, see page 123), the Retire Beckett House (1655), the Hooper-Hathaway House (1662), the Phippen House (c. 1752), and the Counting House (c. 1830).

There are also lovely historic gardens on the property. Both the house and the gardens overlook placid and scenic Salem Harbor.

HOUSE OF THE SEVEN
GABLES

Richard Cavalleri/Shutterstock.com

Hoxie House

16 Water Street
Sandwich, MA 02563
Phone: 508-888-1173

"Post tot naufracia portus. (After so many shipwrecks, a haven.)"
—MOTTO OF THE TOWN OF SANDWICH

The English explorer Bartholomew Gosnold gave Cape Cod its name in 1602, referring to its "great store of codfish." The Mayflower's pilgrims set foot on Cape Cod at Provincetown before making their permanent settlement in Plymouth.

Sandwich is the oldest European settlement on the Cape. It was founded in 1637 and named for Sandwich, England, and it has nothing to do with the sandwich one eats. A century after this town was founded, the Earl of Sandwich popularized the food item. In the 1800s the town became well-known for its pressed glass, an industry which continues to this day.

Hoxie House dates to about 1675. It is one of the oldest houses on Cape Cod and one of the oldest in the Commonwealth of Massachusetts. It was built for the Reverend John Smith, who lived here with his wife and their thirteen children. In the mid-nineteenth century it was bought by Abraham Hoxie, a whaling captain. The town acquired Hoxie House in the 1950s, restored it, and maintains it as a museum.

This is a wood-frame saltbox house, typical of early New England dwellings, which have a long pitched roof that slopes to the back. Such dwellings resemble a lidded wooden box in which salt would have been stored. It is thought that the saltbox house was created when a lean-to was added to the back of a Cape Cod–style house. It is also thought the diminutive lean-to, a single-story addition, may have been selected so as to save on property taxes, but this is conjecture.

Hoxie House has furniture and artifacts dating to the seventeenth century. The house is set in one of the picturesque neighborhoods on Cape Cod.

General Artemas Ward House Museum

786 Main Street
Shrewsbury, MA 01545
Phone: 508-842-8900
www.wardhouse.harvard.edu

"... universally esteemed, beloved and confided in by his army and his country."

—JOHN ADAMS, SPEAKING OF ARTEMAS WARD

At Ward Circle in Washington, DC, there is a monument to Artemas Ward. Its inscription succinctly recounts the life of the man. It reads:

Artemas Ward

1727-1800

Son of Massachusetts

Graduate of Harvard College

Judge and Legislator

Delegate 1780-1781 to

The Continental Congress

Soldier of Three Wars

First Commander of the

Patriot Forces

This house was home to Artemas for much of his life. His parents, Nahim (1684–1754) and Martha Ward (1687–1755), came to Shrewsbury in 1717 and built this house in 1727. It came into the hands of the General in 1763. With a growing family, Artemas doubled the size of the house in 1785. In turn, his son Thomas Walter Ward added an ell to the back in 1820. The family continued to live in the house until 1909. This farm was the family homestead for five generations. In 1925 a great-grandson of the general gave it and a $4 million endowment to Harvard University, which maintains the property and museum.

Naumkeag

5 Prospect Hill Road

Stockbridge, MA 01262

Phone: 413-298-8138 (in-season)

413-298-3239, ext. 3008 (off-season)

www.thetrustees.org/places-to-visit/berkshires/naumkeag.html

The builder of Naumkeag, Joseph Hodges Choate (1832–1917), was born in Salem, Massachusetts, and he named this estate for the native tribe there. Choate was an attorney based in New York City and was one of the founders of the Metropolitan Museum of Art. He was also a diplomat, serving as the United States Ambassador to the Court of St. James from 1899 to 1905 during the reigns of Queen Victoria and King Edward VII.

Choate bought this site in 1884 and in 1886 commissioned Stanford White (1853–1906) to build and furnish his summer home. White created a Shingle-style design with stone and brick towers, a large porch, and large gables. Enlarged twice (at the end of the nineteenth century and again at the beginning of the twentieth), Naumkeag is a forty-four-room house fitted with fine woodwork. White and the Choates toured Europe together on what was essentially a shopping spree to acquire antiques for the house. The house is filled with family heirlooms, among them furniture, Chinese porcelains, and European, American, and Asian art.

After the death of her mother in 1929, Miss Mabel Choate (1870–1958) inherited the house. She summered here until her own death, bequeathing the intact estate to The Trustees for Reservations.

Eight of the property's forty-eight acres are gardens. These were originally planned by Nathan Barrett (1845–1919) in the 1880s. Miss Choate made a significant contribution from 1926 to 1956, working with landscape architect Fletcher Steele (1885–1971) to expand and redesign the outdoor space. The terraced gardens include the Evergreen Garden, the Chinese Garden, the Rose Garden, the Afternoon Garden, the Tree Peony Terrace, and Steele's 1938 addition with its fountain pools, the Blue Steps. Beyond the gardens are forty acres of meadows, woodland, and views of Monument Mountain.

Chesterwood

4 Williamsville Road
Stockbridge, MA 01262
Phone: 413-298-3579
http://chesterwood.org

Stockbridge is a picture-perfect New England town immortalized in paintings by one of its residents, Norman Rockwell (1894–1978). Set along the banks of the Housatonic River in the Berkshire Hills, the town was established by Englishmen in 1734 as a Christian mission to the local Native population. The missionaries called it Indian Town. It was incorporated and renamed for Stockbridge, in Hampshire, England, in 1739. In the nineteenth and twentieth centuries Stockbridge became a haven for writers and artists, Daniel Chester French (1850–1931) among them.

French was born in Exeter, New Hampshire. When he was seventeen years old his family moved to Concord, Massachusetts, where they were friends and neighbors with Ralph Waldo Emerson and the family of Louis May Alcott, whose homes are featured elsewhere in this book. A budding sculptor, French created Concord's Minute Man statue in 1874 in advance of the centenary of the Battle of Lexington and Concord, and that work propelled his artistic career. His best known work is the statue of the seated Abraham Lincoln at the Lincoln Memorial in Washington, DC. While French created the statue in 1920, architect Henry Bacon (1866–1924) designed the building. This was not unusual. The two men worked together on many projects and were not only professional colleagues but also friends.

French lived in New York City. In 1896 he bought this 150-acre farm to be his summer home and retreat. On it there was an 1820 farmhouse. French had it demolished and hired Henry Bacon to design a new house and a studio. The house was constructed in 1901. It is a Georgian Revival work, with a hip roof pierced with gable dormers and topped by a low balustrade. Both house and studio have exterior walls covered with stucco mixed with marble chips. From the house's broad terrace, there are views of the Taconic Mountains.

French found the woodwork in the original 1820 farmhouse reminiscent of that in his family's New Hampshire home. He salvaged the woodwork and paneled the walls of his study with it.

DANIEL CHESTER FRENCH IN
CHESTERWOOD STUDIO (1925)
WITH HIS MODEL FOR THE
STATUE FOR THE LINCOLN
MEMORIAL, WASHINGTON, DC
Chapin Library, Williams College, Gift of the
National Trust for Historic Preservation/
Chesterwood

The artist spent half of each year in Stockbridge, and in this studio he created about two hundred works, including his statue for Washington's Lincoln Memorial. His plaster sketches of it and many other works are on display here.

Margaret French Cresson (1889–1973) inherited Chesterwood from her father in 1931. She formed the Daniel Chester French Foundation to manage the property.

In addition to the house and studio, there is a nineteenth-century barn that houses the visitor center and gallery. Beyond these, be sure to explore the property with its gardens landscaped by French and the fields and forests accessible by walking paths.

Houses of Old Sturbridge Village

1 Old Sturbridge Road
Sturbridge, MA 01566
Phone: 800-733-1830
www.osv.org

Old Sturbridge Village has its roots in the mid-1920s. Three brothers, all heirs to the American Optical Company fortune, began to collect what later became the nucleus of the village. J. Cheney Wells collected clocks, his brother Channing M. favored antique furniture, and the third brother, Albert B., acquired New England antiques. By 1935 the brothers wished to combine their collections and display them to the public. The Wells Historical Museum was founded. The brothers decided to put together a village of historical buildings. The site chosen was David Wright's farm. The farm was developed in the 1840s and included an old mill. By 1941 the Fitch House, the Parsonage, and the Miner Grant Store had been brought here. Old Sturbridge Village has grown to include fifty-nine antique buildings, a working farm, and three water-powered mills on two hundred acres. It is New England's largest living history museum and is staffed by costumed interpreters who present the village as it might have been in the years between 1790 and 1830.

The Bixby House

The Bixby house began its life in Barre Four Corners, Massachusetts, around 1808. The Bixby family lived in this house from the 1820s to the 1870s. It later belonged to the Derby family, who donated it to Old Sturbridge Village in 1974. A relative newcomer to the neighborhood, the house was brought to Sturbridge in 1986 and has since been thoroughly researched and restored.

This white farmhouse has shutters which are painted the original "Paris" green. Inside, the walls, fireplaces, and windows are original, as are many of the furnishings and objects. Emerson Bixby was a blacksmith, and today visitors may see a blacksmith at work.

The Fitch House

This was one of the first houses brought to Old Sturbridge Village soon after its founding in the 1930s. It had been built about 1737 in Willamantic,

Connecticut for a country printer. This is a very charming little house with a gambrel roof and a rose trellis by the front door, all surrounded by a white picket fence. This was originally a smaller house, and additions were made until about 1820. The first floor has five rooms and contains many period pieces.

Among the outbuildings, the corn crib dates to about 1790–1820 and originally was in Scituate, Rhode Island. The barn, though newer, is true to the period, and within there is an exhibit of agricultural equipment and tools.

The Freeman Farm

This diminutive farmhouse (c. 1808) is a one-and-a-half-story gambrel building. It is original to the town of Sturbridge, and so it did not have to travel far to this site in 1950. The outbuildings include the barn, built in Charlton, Massachusetts, around 1840. This is a fine example of a New England–style barn, where the door at one gable end leads to the cattle, while the door at the opposite end leads to the hay. The corn crib is from Thomaston, Connecticut (c. 1830–c. 1860), and the smokehouse, which is from Goshen, Connecticut, dates to about 1800.

Pliny Freeman, his wife Delia, and their seven children all shared in work and chores on the farm. In like manner, today this is a working farm where visitors may see the animals in the barnyards, cooking being done at the kitchen hearth, crops being planted and reaped, and the making of butter and cheese.

The Parsonage

This was one of the first historic buildings brought to Old Sturbridge Village. It arrived here in 1940 after a journey from East Brookfield, Massachusetts. This is the Solomon Richardson House, a lean-to dwelling dating to about 1748. Here it is presented as the Parsonage, or minister's house, and it is furnished with antique decorative arts that are true to the period. The barn is from New York State. Constructed around 1800, it was brought to Sturbridge in 1937.

The Salem Towne House

Here is a large house that belonged to a prosperous family. Built around 1796, it was the Charlton, Massachusetts, home of Salem Towne. His son Salem Jr. inherited the property in 1825. He, his wife Sally, their nine children, hired help, and some visiting relatives lived here. To support the household, Salem wore many hats. He was a "progressive" farmer, land surveyor, businessman, and justice of the peace.

This Federal-style white house has a hipped roof, green door and shutters, and a fan light over the front door. There are four rooms on each floor. The entrance hall leads to a carpeted staircase, and upstairs there was originally a Masonic hall, its walls covered with murals. The Masonic hall was later divided into two bedrooms. Other walls have period wallpaper, and the entire house is furnished with fine decor: carpets, curtains, furniture, ceramics, and other objects, some of which were imported from Europe or Asia. The owners spared no expense in outfitting the kitchen, either. It has a cast-iron stove, which was a luxury in the 1830s.

The property has a formal garden and beyond that an apple orchard, cider mill, and barn.

Stonehurst

100 Robert Treat Paine Drive
Waltham, MA 02453
Phone: 781-314-3290
http://stonehurstwaltham.org/

Stonehurst is also known as the Robert Treat Paine Estate. Paine (1835–1910), whose great-grandfather was a signer of the Declaration of Independence, was a successful Boston lawyer and an investor. He was also a philanthropist, a social reformer, and an advocate for better housing for low- and middle-income people.

Paine was married to Lydia Lyman Paine (1837–1897). Her parents owned the Lyman Estate (1793), which neighbors Stonehurst. When Robert and Lydia wed, they were given a portion of the Lyman Estate on which to build their summer home. Similar gifts were made to other family members. The intent was to form a Lyman family summer compound. Robert and Lydia built a wooden Second Empire house on the site in 1866. After seven children were born, the house was thought to be too small for their needs, and so it was replaced with the present mansion in 1885. They named the estate Stonehurst: The land has many stones, both large and small, and "hurst" is an Old English word for a hill with woods.

Robert had been chairman of the building committee for Trinity Church Copley Square, which was designed in 1872 by Henry Hobson Richardson (1838–1886). Familiar with Richardson's work, Paine hired him to design this Shingle Style house. Its interior has an open plan and is fitted with finely carved woodwork. Both Richardson and the landscape architect Frederick Law Olmsted (1822–1903) (see page 64) were frequent collaborators on projects, and they also worked together here. In fact, this was their only residential joint work.

After Robert and Lydia died, their eldest son, also named Robert Treat Paine (1866–1961), continued to live here. He died at the age of ninety-six. A nephew, Theodore Lyman Storer, donated the 109-acre estate to the City of Waltham in 1974 to be used as a public park. Another Olmsted masterpiece, the park has meadows, woods, rocky outcrops, and trails including the Western Greenway Trail.

The neighboring Lyman Estate (also known as The Vale) is a property of Historic New England, which opens the house for tours (www.historic newengland.org).

Gore Place

52 Gore Street
Waltham, MA 02453
Phone: 781-894-2798
http://goreplace.org

To see a large manor house reminiscent of those found in the countryside of merry old England, look no further. This was the property of Bostonian Christopher Gore (1758–1827), a one-time governor and US senator. He bought the four-hundred-acre property in 1786 and built a wooden summer home, which burned in 1799. Then in 1805 he began to build this, a more fireproof Federal design. The cost was $23,000, and many of the building materials were imported from (you've probably guessed it) England. The architect's name has been lost, but it can be said with certainty that the architect was heavily influenced by the work of Sir John Sloane (1753–1837).

This house was the scene of many large and lavish parties. Hosted here were the Marquis de Lafayette (1757–1834), President James Monroe (1758–1831), and Daniel Webster (1782–1852).

Christopher Gore died in 1827, and his wife passed away in 1834. The contents of the house were sold at auction. The estate had a series of owners until 1921, when it became the Waltham Country Club. The house was surrounded with amenities like a golf course and tennis courts. That chapter came to an end with the Great Depression. Neglected, the house deteriorated. In 1935 it was threatened with demolition, and the property was to be subdivided for suburban houses. Fortunately the Gore Place Society intervened, bought the house and immediate surrounding acres, restored it, and opened it for tours.

The building materials are red brick, and the roof is slate. The main block of the mansion is two-and-a-half stories, with the wings on either end standing at one-and-a-half stories. One wing was the living quarters for the family and the other the living and work areas for the servants. The original wood carriage house (1793) survived the 1799 fire and is also open to visitors.

The Edward Gorey House

8 Strawberry Lane
Yarmouth Port, MA 02675
Phone: 508-362-3909
www.edwardgoreyhouse.org

"To take my work seriously would be the height of folly."

"The helpful thought for which you look
Is written somewhere in a book . . ."

"Books. Cats. Life is good."

— EDWARD GOREY

If you've seen the PBS series *Mystery!* and *Masterpiece Mystery!*, you're familiar with the best known work of Edward St. John Gorey (1925–2000). Each episode began with an animated presentation of Gorey's drawings, and host Vincent Price welcomed viewers to "The Gorey Mansion."

Gorey's work was often evocative of the Victorian and Edwardian worlds, and could be labeled as surrealistic. Gorey was born in Chicago but lived most of his professional life in New York City. He was not only an artist and illustrator but also an author, a playwright, a scenery and costume designer for Broadway shows, and a Tony Award winner. He was as eccentric as he was creative.

In 1979 Gorey bought this house. More than two hundred years old, this sea captain's cottage is also known as The Elephant House. Gorey surrounded himself with the books and cats he loved, and filled his home with his artistic creations and many of his favorite objects.

Gorey lived here until his death in 2000. Two years later it was bought with funds from the Highland Street Foundation, and today it functions as a museum that mounts exhibits of Gorey's work and sponsors traveling exhibits. The mission of the museum is not only to present the artist's home and creative genius, but also to raise awareness of animal rights throughout the world. Gorey would be well-pleased.

NEW HAMPSHIRE

Shaker Dwelling House, Canterbury Shaker Village

288 Shaker Road

Canterbury, NH 03224

Phone: 603-783-9511

www.shakers.org

"When true simplicity is gained,

To bow and to bend we

Shan't be ashamed.

"To turn, turn, will be our delight,

Til by turning, turning

We come 'round right."

—ELDER JOSEPH, "SIMPLE GIFTS"

In recent times there has been an increased interest in Shaker furniture, architecture, and history, as well as the Shakers' simple way of living. The United Society of Believers in Christ's Second Coming began in eighteenth-century England. An offshoot of the Quakers, they were first known as "Shaking Quakers" because of their ecstatic worship. The Shakers lived a celibate life in community.

The Shaker community at Canterbury began in 1792. Their numbers grew. By 1850 there were about three hundred members living and working in one hundred buildings. The trend then reversed. The last male Shaker in Canterbury died in 1939, and the last female died in 1992 at the age of ninety-six. Canterbury Shaker Village is a museum today. Set on nearly seven hundred acres, there are gardens, forests, and fields for visitors to explore and enjoy. Twenty-five of the buildings are original and four have been reconstructed. The largest of these is the Dwelling House. The oldest part of the house dates to 1793. As the community grew, so did the Dwelling House. The final addition was made in 1837. There were separate areas for bedrooms for the men and the women. The Dwelling House has a common room, dining room, kitchen, and baking room, as well as a chapel in which there are concerts today.

Saint-Gaudens National Historic Site

139 Saint Gaudens Road
Cornish, NH 03745
Phone: 603-675-2175
https://www.nps.gov/saga

"What garlic is to salad, insanity is to art."

—AUGUSTUS SAINT-GAUDENS

Augustus Saint-Gaudens (1848–1907) was one of America's greatest sculptors. Born in Dublin to an Irish mother and a French father, he and his family immigrated to America within a few months of his birth, settling in New York City. His first job was in a cameo cutter's factory. He studied art in New York and, at the age of nineteen, went to Europe where he studied in Paris and Rome. It was in Rome that he met his American wife, Augusta Fisher Homer (1848–1926).

Some of Saint-Gaudens's best known works are the equestrian William Tecumseh Sherman memorial at the entrance to New York's Central Park at Fifth Avenue and Fifty-Ninth Street, the Robert Gould Shaw Memorial in Boston Common opposite the Massachusetts State House, the veiled and mysterious seated figure at the Adams Memorial in Washington's Rock Creek Cemetery, a statue of Diana (the original of which once topped Stanford White's Madison Square Garden in New York), and the gold "Double Eagle" twenty-dollar coin, thought to be the most beautiful American coin ever minted.

Saint-Gaudens was a member of the Cornish Art Colony. Begun in 1885, the colony here and in other nearby Connecticut River Valley towns was a cluster of more than one hundred artists and designers. Augustus bought Huggins' Folly, a brick Federal-style inn dating to the early 1800s, and made it his summer home, naming it Aspet after his father's hometown in France. Working with architect George Fletcher Babb (1836–1915), Saint-Gaudens added dormers and surrounded the house with pergolas and porches from which there are views of Mount Ascutney.

Augustus also built studios and designed terraced gardens. Both the studios and gardens are the settings for more than one hundred of his sculptures. Augustus and Augusta summered here from 1885 to 1897. He then lived here year round until his death in 1907. When Augusta died in 1926, she bequeathed the estate and its original furnishings to the Saint-Gaudens Memorial, which made it into a museum. The Memorial then gave the property to the National Park Service in 1965. Other than a portion of the Appalachian National Scenic Trail, this is New Hampshire's only National Park Service site.

The Robert Frost Farm

122 Rockingham Road
Derry, NH 03038
Phone: 603-432-3091
www.robertfrostfarm.org

"Two roads converged in a yellow wood,
And sorry I could not travel both
And be one traveler, long I stood
And looked down one as far as I could
To where it bent in the undergrowth;

"Then took the other, as just as fair,
And having perhaps the better claim,
Because it was grassy and wanted wear;
Though as for that the passing there
Had worn them really about the same,

"And both that morning equally lay
In leaves no step had trodden black.
Oh, I kept the first for another day!
Yet knowing how way leads on to way,
I doubted if I should ever come back.

"I shall be telling this with a sigh
Somewhere ages and ages hence:
Two roads diverged in a wood, and I –
I took the one less traveled by,
And that has made all the difference."

—ROBERT FROST, "THE ROAD NOT TAKEN"

Robert Frost (1874–1963) is one of the most popular twentieth-century American poets. His poems convey the spirit of New England rural life, and it was at this farm that he was inspired to write many of them, including "The Road Not Taken." He was awarded the Pulitzer Prize for Poetry and the Congressional Gold Medal.

But Frost did not always live here. He and his family moved here from

Lawrence, Massachusetts, in 1900. Here he wrote most of his poems for his books *Mountain Interval, North of Boston*, and *A Boy's Will*. The Frosts left the farm in 1909 when Robert began teaching, first at Pinkerton Academy and later at Plymouth Normal School. Funds from his sale of the farm in 1911 paid for his family's journey to England, where his poetic genius was recognized and his first book was published.

Following this, the farm had several owners. Sadly, it degenerated to an automobile grave in the 1960s. Frost expressed his wish that the farm be bought and restored to what it had been. He never lived to see this; he died in 1962. The State of New Hampshire bought the farm in 1974 and restored it. The Robert Frost Farm is a New Hampshire State Park.

Visitors may tour the parlor, dining room, kitchen, pantry, laundry room, and bedrooms. There are also a barn and woodshed to see and trails to explore. The Park also offers poetry readings.

ROBERT FROST FARM

Zach Frank / Shutterstock.com

Zimmerman House

Currier Museum of Art
150 Ash Street
Manchester, NH 03104
Phone: 603-669-6144
www.currier.org/collections/zimmerman-house/

> *"Every great architect is—necessarily—a great poet. He must be a*
> *great original interpreter of his time, his day, his age."*
>
> —FRANK LLOYD WRIGHT

The name Frank Lloyd Wright (1867–1959) is synonymous with great twentieth-century American architecture. Wright championed organic architecture in harmony with the environment and humanity.

The Zimmerman House is a fine example of Wright's "usonian" houses: dwellings of a modest size, occupying a single floor, concrete floors with radiant heat rising from them, and clerestory windows. Wright's first usonian homes were built in 1936. This house was built for Dr. Isadore and Lucille Zimmerman in 1950. Wright designed not only the house but also its furnishing and fabrics, overlooking no detail, from the mailbox to the placemats! The Zimmermans left their home to the Currier Art Museum in 1988. It contains items from their art collection.

Special note: The Zimmerman House is located at 223 Heather Street in Manchester, but it is accessed for tours by van from the Currier Museum of Art. Reservations are required.

INTERIOR OF THE
ZIMMERMAN HOUSE

Photo Jeffrey Nintzel, courtesy
of the Currier Museum of Art

The Fells

456 Route 103A
Newbury, NH 03255
Phone: 603-763-4789
www.thefells.org

Resembling the high, rocky pastures in the northern reaches of Scotland, the Hay estate came to be known as The Fells. It was the summer home and retreat of John Milton Hay (1838–1905) and three generations of his family. Hay was the private secretary and assistant to Abraham Lincoln and was at the president's deathbed. He served as secretary of state under Presidents William McKinley and Theodore Roosevelt, and he was the US ambassador to Great Britain. He was also an author, a biographer, and a poet. Seeking an escape from the stifling summer heat of Washington, Hay bought one thousand acres on the shores of Lake Sunapee in 1888. And on the lake he had two rustic houses built in 1891 and 1897, one for him and his family and the other for guests. The houses were connected by a breezeway. Teddy Roosevelt was a guest here in 1902 and planted a maple tree which came to be known as "The Roosevelt Tree."

John's son Clarence Hay (1884–1969) inherited the house in 1905. Ten years later he and his wife, Alice Appleton Hay (1894–1987), combined the two small, rustic houses, added to them, and transformed them into the Colonial Revival design we see today, with its white exterior, porch, dormers, and gambrel roof. The interior is decorated with paneling and scenic wallpapers. The Hays also cultivated the gardens: the rock garden, the rose terrace, the perennial border, the heather bed, and the old garden.

Clarence died in 1969, and Alice passed away in 1987. The house was restored in the 1990s and opened to the public for viewing. Visitors are welcome to explore the scenic trails of the John Hay National Wildlife Refuge, which is on a hillside overlooking Lake Sunapee.

Barrett House

79 Main Street
New Ipswich, NH 03071
Phone: 603-878-2517
www.historicnewengland.org/historic-properties/homes/
barrett-house/barrett-house

First known as Forest Hall, this Federal house was built around 1800. It was commissioned by Charles Barrett Sr. (1740–1808), a very prosperous man who owned New Hampshire's first cotton mill and who also invested in canals and toll roads. He built this as a wedding gift for his son Charles Jr. (1773–1836) and Martha Minot. By 1887 this had become a summer home, and in 1950 it was presented to what is now known as Historic New England. An interesting aside: the movie *The Europeans*, starring Lee Remick, was filmed here in 1979.

The interior of Barrett House is delightfully frozen in time, with French scenic wallpapers, other wallpapers, and original fine furnishings. The third floor has a ballroom with musical instruments that are true to the period. This is a seventy-acre property planted with flower gardens. Not to be missed at the back of the house are the flight of steps and allée leading up the hill to an enchanting Gothic Revival trellised summer house.

DINING ROOM MANTEL,

BARRETT HOUSE

Courtesy of Historic New

England

Governor John Langdon House

143 Pleasant Street
Portsmouth, New Hampshire 03801
Phone: 603-436-3203
http://www.historicnewengland.org/property/
governor-john-langdon-house/

Portsmouth has the distinction of being New Hampshire's oldest settlement and its only seaport. Founded as a fishing center along the shore of the Piscataqua River in 1623, the town was first named for the river, later changing its name to the more picturesque "Strawbery Banke." In 1653 the town was incorporated and named for Portsmouth, England. With its thriving harbor, Portsmouth was an English provincial capital in colonial times and later became New Hampshire's first state capital. An important part of the local economy has been the Naval Shipyard, which opened in 1790.

John Langdon (1741–1819) was a delegate to the Constitutional Convention and a signer of the United States Constitution. He served in the Continental Congress, was a US senator (New Hampshire's first) and served three terms as governor of New Hampshire. He was also a shipbuilder and a merchant.

This house was completed in 1785. President George Washington visited this house and, among Portsmouth houses, deemed it "the first." The design is typical of late Georgian houses: a facade five bays across, a hipped roof pierced by three dormers and crowned by a balustrade. Within, the entrance hall is exceptionally large, as are the reception rooms, which are embellished with finely carved Rococo woodwork. In the garden there is a pavilion, a 150-foot-long arbor, and flower beds.

When the Governor died in 1819, the house went to his daughter, and it later had a series of owners. It was sold back to Langdon family descendants in 1877. In 1906 they hired the firm of McKim, Mead, & White to add a two-story wing, a dining room, and modern amenities. The house was transformed into a fine example of the Colonial Revival style. The last descendant to own the house was Elizabeth Langdon, who in 1947 gifted it to the Society for the Preservation of New England Antiquities (Historic New England) which preserves and displays two other historic properties in Portsmouth: Jackson House (1664) and Rundlett-May House (1807).

GOVERNOR JOHN
LANGDON HOUSE
ENTRY HALL AND
STAIRS
Courtesy of Historic New
England

Moffatt-Ladd House and Garden

154 Market Street

Portsmouth, NH 03801

Phone: 603-436-8221, 603-430-7968

www.moffattladd.org

The wealthiest man in colonial New Hampshire, John Moffatt (1691–1786), had this house built in 1763 as a wedding gift for his son Samuel. Samuel and his bride lived here for a short time. His father then moved into this, the house he had built, and lived here with his daughter Catharine and her husband William Whipple (1730–1785). Whipple signed the Declaration of Independence and was a brigadier general during the American Revolution. His portrait, sword, and other personal items are here. John Moffatt lived to be ninety-five years old, dying in 1786. The property eventually (in 1818) went to one of his granddaughters, Maria Tufton Haven Ladd. Her son Alexander Hamilton Ladd, in turn, lived here and cultivated the fine gardens. Alexander died in 1900, and in 1911 his heirs gave the house and gardens to the National Society of Colonial Dames in New Hampshire, which owns and maintains the property today.

This is a Georgian house with a unique floor plan. There is no central hall, but rather the great hall and staircase are in a corner of the house. The immense, beautifully crafted soffit under the grand staircase is carved from a single piece of wood. The Parisian wallpaper on the first and second floors depicts a 360-degree view of Naples. On the third floor there is the children's nursery with its original toys. The tour progresses up the grand staircase and down the servants' stairs.

The garden covers two acres. Of special note is the towering and massive chestnut tree planted by William Whipple in 1776 with seeds he brought back from Philadelphia. Also dating to the eighteenth century are the garden's damask rose bushes. There are several outbuildings, the most noteworthy being the wood warehouse. It originally was across the street on the family's wharf, and it was moved here around 1812.

Houses of Strawbery Banke

14 Hancock Street
Portsmouth, NH 03801
Phone: 603-433-1100
www.strawberybanke.org

Strawbery Banke is a ten-acre neighborhood of historic houses and other buildings spanning four centuries. There are about forty buildings and nearly all of them are on their original sites. Dating to 1639, this was the first European settlement in New Hampshire. It was founded by Captain Walter Neale (1618–1639). The area was aptly (and picturesquely) named for the profusion of wild strawberries that spread here near the shores of the Piscataqua River. In the eighteenth century this was a bustling neighborhood of shipbuilding and maritime trade, in the nineteenth century it was populated with European immigrants, and by the mid-twentieth century the neighborhood was a mix of tenements, houses, businesses, and scrapyards. Puddle Dock, as the neighborhood was also called because of its saltwater inlet, was slated to fall to the wrecking ball in the name of urban renewal. Preservationists saved Puddle Dock from this fate in 1958, and Strawbery Banke was first opened as a museum in 1965. It has become a model for the preservation, restoration, and adaptive reuse of historic structures.

Strawbery Banke is a living history museum with costumed interpreters. There are mansions, working-class homes, and tenement houses from the seventeenth, eighteenth, nineteenth, and mid-twentieth centuries, as well as businesses, farm buildings, and taverns (visited by George Washington, the Marquis de Lafayette, and other notables). Visitors may see an historic greenhouse, an apple orchard, and several gardens as cultivated from the seventeenth century up through the twentieth (a World War II Victory Garden) and into the present (community gardens).

Warner House

150 Daniel Street
Portsmouth, NH 03802
Phone: 603-436-5909
http://warnerhouse.org

Over three hundred years old, the Warner House is the oldest brick house in a northern New England city. Its bricks were made in New Hampshire and laid in a Flemish bond, forming walls that are two and a half feet thick. Archibald Macpheadris (1680–1729) a Scotch-Irish sea captain, commissioned this house in 1716. When he died, it went to his widow (née Sarah Wentworth) and their children. Sarah then married merchant George Jaffrey (for whom Jaffrey, New Hampshire, is named) and moved a few doors down the street to his house. Sarah's brother, the Royal Governor Benning Wentworth, then moved into this house and lived here for twenty years. Benning's daughter married Jonathan Warner in 1760. In the 1880s this became the summer home for the Wentworth descendants. By the 1930s, the neighborhood had declined and the family wished to sell. They got an offer from an oil company that wanted to demolish the house and put a service station on the site. Fortunately the Warner House Association was formed and saved the house by purchasing it for $10,000 in 1932—no small feat during the Great Depression. It subsequently opened as a museum, and over the years it has been restored and many original furnishings, books, china, and ephemera have been returned to the house.

This is an early Georgian house, and the floor plan is typical of houses of the period: a large central hall flanked by four large rooms. The walls of the great hall are embellished with murals dating to 1718. While some of the subjects depicted remain a mystery, it is definite that two Mohawk sachems flank the window on the staircase landing. The dining room has a series of family portraits by Joseph Blackburn (d. 1787), a mentor to John Singleton Copley (1738–1815). Overall, this is an outstanding and dignified colonial house.

Wentworth Lear Historic Houses

50 Mechanic Street
Portsmouth, NH 03801
Phone: 603-436-4406
http://wentworthlear.org

The Wentworth-Gardner House and the Tobias Lear House are neighboring dwellings. Both are owned and operated by the Wentworth-Gardner and Tobias Lear Houses Association.

The Wentworth House was built as a wedding gift. Mark Hunking Wentworth (1712–1785) and his wife Elizabeth built this Georgian mansion in 1760. Their son Thomas and his bride Anne Tasker were the recipients of the gift. The Wentworths were kin to Governor Benning Wentworth, who lived at the Warner House (see page 156). In 1793 Major William Gardner (c.1751–1834) bought the house and lived in it for forty years until his death at the age of eighty-three. When the area deteriorated this became an apartment and boarding house. Antiquarian and photographer Wallace Nutting (1861–1941) bought the house in 1915 and made it a Colonial Revival showpiece. In turn, the Metropolitan Museum of Art bought the house and planned to move it to New York City, possibly to Central Park, but their plans were foiled by the Great Depression. In 1940 the Association bought the house and today maintains it as a museum.

The exterior of this wood-frame house has five bays, decorative quoins at the corners, and a hip roof with three dormers. Passing through the elaborate doorframe, visitors enter the great hall, which runs the length of the house; the rooms are embellished with exquisite hand-carved woodwork.

The Tobias Lear House is also Georgian. It was constructed in 1749 for Captain Tobias Lear III (1706–1751). His grandson, Tobias Lear V (1762–1816), was the private secretary to President George Washington, who visited Mrs. Mary Lear and her family in her home in 1789. The house remained in the family until 1860 when it was divided into apartments. As with the Wentworth-Gardner house, this home was acquired by Wallace Nutting and ultimately by the Association.

RHODE ISLAND

ENTRANCE TO
BLITHEWOLD MANSION

Courtesy of Blithewold Mansion,
Gardens, and Arboretum

Blithewold

101 Ferry Road
Bristol, RI 02809
Phone: 401-253-2707
www.blithewold.org

The estate known as Blithewold enjoys an idyllic setting along the shore of Narragansett Bay. The house we see today is the second on this site. Augustus Van Wickle (1856–1898), a Pennsylvania coal magnate, and his wife Bessie (1860–1936) had a Queen Anne–style house built here in 1896. Augustus only enjoyed two summers here, as he died in a hunting accident in 1898. Three years later, his widow married William McKee.

The summer home was destroyed by fire in 1906. Fortunately, its contents were saved. The stucco and stone English Country Manor house we see today was designed by Walter Kilham and built in 1907.

Augustus and Bessie had two daughters: Marjorie and Augustine. Marjorie died at Blithewold in 1976 at the age of ninety-three. She left the estate and an endowment to the Heritage Trust of Rhode Island, and Blithewold was opened to the public in 1978.

Visitors approach the house by way of a Chinese moon gate. Blithewold Mansion has forty-five rooms. These cover a wide spectrum of revival styles, which run the gamut from Tudor to American colonial. Nearly all of them have views of the bay. Personal favorites are the paneled dining room and billiards room and the light and airy breakfast porch. The self-guided tour includes the first and second floors.

This is a thirty-three-acre property. The gardens include a greenhouse, an arboretum, more than five hundred species of woody plants, a bamboo grove, rose garden, rock garden, and water garden. Of special note is the largest giant sequoia on the East Coast. In April the Blithewold estate is abloom with thousands of daffodils.

Linden Place

500 Hope Street
Bristol, RI 02809
Phone: 401-253-0390
www.lindenplace.org

"The Mansion," as Linden Place was long known, is a beautiful house. It was built in 1810, though unfortunately its builder, George DeWolf (1779–1844), has a dubious history. He was a seafarer, a general, and a slave trader. When his fortunes reversed in 1825, he left The Mansion (and Bristol) in the middle of the night. The property went on to a series of other DeWolf family members. By 1853 the house was a hotel and boarding house. Things began to look up when, in 1865, George DeWolf's daughter Theodora (1820–1901) was given the house by her son Edward Colt (1844–1868), nephew of Samuel Colt (1814–1862) of firearms fame. After Theodora's death in 1901, the house passed to her son Samuel P. Colt. Twenty years later he died, leaving the property in trust to his grandchildren. In 1989 the last of his grandchildren, Elizabeth Colt Stansfield, sold the estate to the Friends of Linden Place for $1.5 million. Five generations of DeWolfs and Colts had lived in this house.

The architect hired by George DeWolf was Russell Warren (1783–1860). A Rhode Island native, Warren built many Federal-style and Greek Revival buildings in Providence, Bristol, and other places in New England. This is a wooden Federal-style house. The façade is dominated by four towering Corinthian columns. Above the entry door there is a fan light, and a second fan light sits over the window above that. The great hall leads to a spiral staircase. The most charming and distinctive feature of Linden Place is the octagonal, light-filled Gothic Revival conservatory, added by Russell Warren in the 1850s. The beautiful wrought-iron fence was also added at that time. It had been moved here from another house in Somerset, Massachusetts, and probably dates to about 1815–1825.

When Samuel P. Colt inherited the house in 1901, he made many changes to the property. He enclosed the side porches and added a billiard room and modern plumbing. Most notably, he constructed a yellow-brick building which houses a ballroom. The architect was Wallace E. Howe, also of Bristol. Today the ballroom is the site of many wedding receptions, parties, dances, and other events. Those who attend events at Linden Place are in good company. Actress Ethel Barrymore Colt (1879–1959), the "First Lady of the American Theater," was entertained here, as were no fewer than four US presidents.

Samuel P. Colt also lavished attention on the grounds with the addition of more than twenty European sculptures depicting animals and classical Greek and Roman figures. Colt developed a farm at the north end of Bristol which today is Colt State Park. It, like Linden Place, is adorned with statuary collected by Samuel.

Chateau-sur-Mer

474 Bellevue Avenue
Newport, RI 02840
Phone: 401- 847-0037
www.newportmansions.org

Chateau-sur-Mer was home to three generations of the Wetmore family. William Shepard Wetmore (1801–1862) made a fortune in the Old China Trade, exporting porcelains, teas, spices, and silks from China to America. In 1852, at the age of fifty-two, he built this, his retirement home. The property at that time was more than forty acres and extended to the ocean. And so his house came to be known as the Chateau-sur-Mer or "castle by the sea." He did not live to enjoy a long retirement. Ten years after building his chateau, William died. He left the property to his sixteen-year-old son George Peabody Wetmore (1846–1921) and a large inheritance to his fourteen-year-old daughter Annie Derby Rogers Wetmore (1848–1884).

George married Edith Malvina Keteltas (1851–1927) in 1869, and for the next decade they lived in Britain and toured the continent. And it was during this time that their four children—two boys and two girls—were born. George was a graduate of Yale University and Columbia Law School. He served as governor of Rhode Island and represented Rhode Island in the United States Senate.

None of George's children ever married. His last surviving child was Miss Edith Wetmore (1870–1966), who lived to be ninety-five. Following her death, everything in the house was sold at auction and the house was sold to The Preservation Society of Newport County. Members of the Society bought major pieces of furniture at the auction and then donated these pieces to keep in the house. What was not saved through purchase has been replaced with similar items that are true to the period. The house looks very much as it did when the Wetmores lived here.

The house was built for William in 1852 in the then-popular Italianate style, drawing inspiration from the villas and farmhouses of Tuscany. The Italianate style was made fashionable by Queen Victoria with the building of Osborne House on the Isle of Wight in 1845. A fortress-like, mammoth structure, Chateau-sur-Mer was built of granite brought from

CHATEAU-SUR-MER

*Gavin Ashworth photo courtesy
of The Preservation Society of
Newport County*

Fall River, Massachusetts. The contractor Seth Bradford oversaw its construction. When completed, the Chateau was the grandest house in Newport and remained so for forty years until the Gilded Age and the building of larger and more opulent houses like Marble House and the Breakers.

It was enlarged for George. While he and his bride were in Europe during the 1870s, Richard Morris Hunt (1827–1895) redesigned the house, transitioning it from an Italianate villa to a larger Second Empire palace. On the exterior he raised the roof, crowning the house with a straight Mansard design. Hunt added a new entrance with a porte cochère, a second tower, and a three-story wing. On the interior, Hunt gutted the center of the house and created a great hall, which rises forty-five feet. This was his first great hall. Twenty years later he would design great halls on a grander scale in two other Newport mansions: The Breakers and Marble House.

Here under one roof there are a number of interior styles popular in the Victorian Age. The entrance staircase, the great hall, and the reception room are all in the Eastlake style. Charles Locke Eastlake (1836–1906) was a British architect and designer who advocated the use of light woods, simplicity in carving, and spindle work. By contrast, the Italian Renaissance library and dining room are the work of Luigi Frullini (1839–1897), a Florentine master woodcarver, furniture maker, and designer. These are the only two Frullini rooms in America. The ballroom is a mid-nineteenth century design by the Parisian cabinetmaker and designer Leon Marcotte (1824–1887). And the adjoining Green Salon is the work of Ogden Codman Jr. (1863–1951), who with Edith Wharton (see page 94) coauthored the monumental work *The Decoration of Houses*. The bay window in the Marble Hall is the work of architect John Russell Pope (1874–1937), who is best known for designing the Jefferson Memorial in Washington, DC.

The garden reflects the taste in landscape architecture that was popular in the late nineteenth century: a vast lawn planted with rare specimens of trees from around the globe. The Olmsted brothers (see page 64) further enhanced the landscape design in 1915. In the garden there is a Chinese moon gate that dates to 1860. A picturesque addition to the estate, it once framed views of the Atlantic Ocean beyond it.

Chepstow

120 Narragansett Avenue
Newport, RI 02840
Phone: 401-847-0421
www.newportmansions.org

Chepstow was built in 1860 for New Yorker Edmund Schermerhorn (1817–1891). His ancestors were Dutch, and in 1636 they arrived in New Amsterdam, as New York was then known. The family amassed a fortune in real estate. Edmund Schermerhorn at first summered here and later lived in this house year-round.

The property was acquired in 1911 by a member of another established New York family, Mrs. Emily Morris Gallatin. Morris family members were descendants of the Lords of the Manor of Morrisania. The manor was an immense landholding stretching from what is now known as The Bronx, New York, across the Harlem and Hudson Rivers, and into New Jersey. The first British governor of New Jersey was Lewis Morris (1671–1746), and both Morris County and Morristown, New Jersey, are named for him. His grandson, also named Lewis Morris (1726–1798), was a signer of the Declaration of Independence and a delegate to the Continental Congress. Recalling a Welsh castle where Morris ancestors fought during the English Civil War, Mrs. Gallatin named the house Chepstow. She died in 1944, and her husband passed away in 1948. The property was bequeathed to Emily's cousin Lewis Gouverneur Morris and his daughters Alletta and Frances, residents of Park Avenue, New York City.

Alletta (1912–1986), her husband Byrnes MacDonald (1908–1959), and their son George began to summer at Chepstow in 1950. Mr. MacDonald, president of the Standard Oil Company, died in 1959. Four years later Alletta married a second time, this time to Californian Peter McBean. Over the years Alletta gathered Morris family artwork, furnishings, documents, and memorabilia from several houses and brought them together at Chepstow with the intent of opening the house to the public as a museum. When Alletta died in 1986 at the age of seventy-four, she left the house, its contents, and a generous endowment to The Preservation Society of Newport County. She also left the Alletta Morris McBean

Foundation to "enhance the quality of life in, and perpetuate the history of, Newport."

The architect was a Newport man, George Champlin Mason Jr. (1820–1894). He designed more than 150 buildings in this, the "City by the Sea." At Chepstow, Mason used the Italianate style, which was popular in America during the antebellum period. Note the round top windows and door, the large eaves, and the decorative pediments under them. Note also the porch on the right, here known as the piazza. The piazza once wrapped around the house on three sides, later giving way to the library and the sun room. The parquetry floors of the house (in the entrance foyer and dining room) are typical of Mason's interiors. A tour of the first floor includes the foyer, drawing room, sitting room, library, dining room, sun room, and pantry. The tour continues upstairs to the bedrooms, and en route visitors pass a series of nineteenth-century oil paintings depicting views of the Hudson River.

Chepstow contains no fewer than 7,800 objects, all of which are original to the house. The treasures here include family portraits as well as works by Albert Bierstadt, Thomas Sully, James McNeill Whistler, and the Dutch master William van der Velde the Younger. A highlight is *New York Yacht Club Regatta* by Fitz Henry Lane. There is also a series of more contemporary paintings by Cape Cod folk artists Ralph and Martha Cahoon. Most of the furniture dates to the seventeenth, eighteenth, and nineteenth centuries. Alletta MacDonald added her personal touch with her needlepoint on many chairs. Some of her other crafts adorn the house: decoupage, collage, and photomontage. She was a very creative lady! The interior is light-filled and has a refined atmosphere. A personal favorite is the sun room, which was added in the 1960s.

Hunter House

54 Washington Street
Newport, RI 02840
Phone: 401-847-7516
www.newportmansions.org

Hunter House dates to eighteenth-century Newport's Golden Age. This neighborhood is known as The Point because of the long peninsula which once jutted out into the harbor. It was colonial Newport's bustling center, with shops, rum distilleries, warehouses, wharfs, tall ships, and the homes of sea captains and wealthy merchants. One such merchant was Jonathan Nichols (1712–1756). When he built this house in 1748 it was roughly a third the size of what we see today. It was a long, narrow, tall house with one central chimney (roughly the northern third of today's house).

Following the death of Nichols in 1756, the property was acquired by Colonel Joseph Wanton Jr. (1730–1780), also a merchant and a deputy governor. He added the central hall, more rooms, and a second chimney. Wanton had the interior fitted with fine paneling and made this a true Georgian mansion. Wanton was a Tory. When the British evacuated Newport in 1780 Wanton departed also. The comte de Rochambeau (1725–1807), commander in chief of the French Expeditionary Force, came to Newport in 1780, with five thousand French land troops. Admiral Charles-Henri-Louis d'Arsac, chevalier de Ternay (1723–1780), was given this house as his headquarters, and he died under its roof soon after his arrival.

After the American Revolution, the house was bought by Senator William Hunter (1774–1849). As the house remained in his family for a half-century, it is now known as Hunter House. The Hunters sold the house in 1858, and it was then used variously as an apartment house, a rooming house, and, ultimately, a convent. Things changed dramatically in 1945. A major American museum wanted to buy the house, demolish it, and place its exceptionally fine paneling on display in the museum. To prevent its demolition and restore the house, The Preservation Society of Newport County was founded under the leadership of Katherine Warren. Countess Gladys Vanderbilt Szechenyi, heiress to The Breakers (see page

HUNTER HOUSE

jiawangkun/Shutterstock.com

186), agreed to allow visitors to tour the first floor of The Breakers. This proved to be a successful fundraiser, and the income realized financed the restoration of Hunter House, which was opened to the public as a museum in 1953.

Think of Hunter House as a Georgian jewel box, with its furnishings as the jewels within. Sadly, the original contents of the house are long gone. However, today it is filled with English and American period pieces. These furnishings span periods from the Jacobean era through those of the William and Mary, Queen Anne, Chippendale, and Federal Era styles. In eighteenth-century Newport there were over one hundred cabinetmakers who produced furniture for the local market and as venture cargo to be sold from ships visiting ports along the East Coast, but the best of them were the Townsends and Goddards. These Quaker men produced some of the finest furniture ever made in America, working between 1730 and 1820. Some of their best works are on display at Hunter House. Another jewel in the house is an oil painting by Gilbert Stuart (1755–1828). Stuart was a Rhode Island native who is best known for his many portraits of George Washington. A copy of one is on the dollar bill. Here at Hunter House is his first oil painting, created when he was a teenager. It depicts Dr. Hunter's spaniels. (Dr. Hunter was Senator Hunter's father.) It is believed that this may have been painted as payment for medical services.

On the water side of the house, there is a garden overlooking Narragansett Bay. At the street side be sure to see the carved wooden pineapple over the door. The pineapple was a symbol of hospitality throughout the Colonies. When sea captains returned home from long voyages in warmer climates, they would often bring pineapples and other fruits with them. Placing a pineapple over the front door of their home or perhaps on a gatepost signaled to friends and neighbors that they had returned from their voyage and were welcoming visitors. In like manner the pineapple today is a welcoming sign and invitation to Hunter House to see the treasures within.

Isaac Bell House

70 Perry Street

Newport, RI 02840

401-849-1894

www.newportmansions.org

Isaac Bell (1846–1889) was a New Yorker. He supplemented the income from his inheritance with work as a cotton broker and was a major investor in the transatlantic cable. His wife, née Jeanette Bennett, was the heiress to the *New York Herald* fortune. Her brother, James Gordon Bennett Jr., also summered in Newport, and in 1880 he built the Newport Casino (which now houses the International Tennis Hall of Fame, shops, and restaurants). Isaac Bell retired at the age of thirty-one. When in 1881 he decided to build a Newport home for his family, he hired the same architectural firm that had designed the casino. He hired McKim, Mead, and White.

In 1876, the nation celebrated its centennial. That sparked a renewed interest in American colonial architecture. The Isaac Bell house combines styles and influences not only from America's shingled colonial houses, but also from French farmhouses, windmills, and towers. Also, there was much interest in all things Japanese during this period. Some of the details here, both inside and outside, mimic Japanese design. The shingles and the large gables on the house's exterior are American. The tower to the right is similar in form to some French medieval towers, and the tower with the bell-shaped roof near the entrance door is similar to French windmills. Two sea creatures over the porch leading to the front door and the porch columns (which are carved to look like bamboo) are somewhat Japanese in appearance. In similar manner, colonial American, French, and Japanese features are echoed inside the house.

When built, this house was first dubbed "modernized colonial." Later, in the mid-twentieth century, it came to be known as the Shingle Style.

The house was completed in 1883. President Grover Cleveland appointed Bell to the post of minister resident (ambassador) to the Court of the Netherlands in 1886. There he became ill, returned to America, and died in 1889 at the age of forty-two. He and his family had lived in this house for just six years. The house was sold and became home to a series of families and for a period was a nursing home.

In 1994 The Preservation Society of Newport County bought the Isaac Bell House, recognizing its architectural significance. The Society has been meticulously restoring the house since then: first the exterior, then the interior, and finally the decorative wallpapers and furnishings. Visitors see the Bell House as a work in progress. The reception room is known as the "archeology room," as it has not been fully restored. Next is the drawing room, which is restored in part. Work in the dining room and the living hall has been completed. The dining table, dining room carpet, and a bed are original, but there are few other furnishings. The tour continues on to the pantry, and then the kitchen, and then upstairs to the bedrooms.

Kingscote

253 Bellevue Avenue
Newport, RI 02840
Phone: 401-847-0366
www.newportmansions.org

Newport enjoys perhaps the most temperate climate in New England. Buffered by the Atlantic Ocean to the south, Narragansett Bay to the west, and the Sakonnet River to the east, the gentle breezes here have attracted summer visitors for generations. Before the arrival of the Europeans, Native peoples from villages inland would come to this island to do their summer plantings and to harvest crustaceans and fish from the surrounding waters. In colonial times Newport became a haven for Southern families who would sail up the Atlantic coast and summer here. The trend continued after the American Revolution, especially among the wealthy from Georgia and the Carolinas. Escaping humidity, heat, and malaria, they dubbed Newport the "Carolina hospital."

In 1839 a plantation owner from Savannah, George Noble Jones (1811–1876), built the summer home we now know as Kingscote. He chose a site on a hill that was then on the outskirts of town. Bellevue Avenue was a dirt road with another name, and the neighborhood to the south, now populated with grand mansions, was farmland. This property afforded sweeping views of the Atlantic Ocean on one side and Newport Harbor on the other. Jones set a trend. In the early nineteenth century his fellow Southerners would lodge in Newport's large resort hotels. Seeing his summer cottage, others began to build theirs, too. They were "keeping up with the Joneses."

The architect for this *cottage orne*, or decorative cottage, was Richard Upjohn (1802–1878). Born an Englishman, Upjohn came to America. He was a cofounder of the American Institute of Architects in 1857 as well as its first president. He was also a champion of the Gothic Revival style in America. His best known work is Trinity Church, on Wall Street, in New York City (completed in 1846). Gothic Revival buildings drew their inspiration from medieval prototypes. There are many Gothic Revival churches and some "collegiate gothic" school buildings, but relatively few Gothic Revival houses. This is one of them. Some features seen here which are typical of that style are the steeply pitched roofs, windows

KINGSCOTE

Ira Kerns photo courtesy of The
Preservation Society of Newport
County

crowned with pointed tops, gables, dormers, drip moulding over windows and doors, and decorative lattices.

In 1861, at the outbreak of the Civil War, George Noble Jones and his Southern compatriots left Newport and returned home. He left a few of his possessions behind: Gothic Revival chairs and other pieces made by Joseph Meeks of New York, and a pair of fire buckets labeled "N. Jones." The house was acquired by an old Newport family, the Kings. Dr. David King I came to the city in 1799. His descendants later made a fortune in the Old China Trade. The estate came to be known as Kingscote—an abbreviated form of "Kings' Cottage."

In 1881 the Kings hired Stanford White (1853–1906) to add the large dining room and bedrooms above it. White drew from colonial American, British, Oriental, and Italian styles in designing this room, and it is lit by hundreds of glass opalescent bricks created by Louis C. Tiffany & Co.

The last King descendant to live in the house was Mrs. Anthony Barclay (Gwendolen) Rives (1911–1972), who bequeathed the house, its contents, and an endowment to The Preservation Society of Newport County. When the Society acquired the house, it was so overflowing with artwork, family memorabilia, and other treasures that passage through each room was by way of a narrow path. Many of the original objects have been distributed to other Preservation Society houses. What remains here are five thousand objects collected by the King family over five generations. These are from the colonial era, from the Old China Trade, and from travels in Europe.

The property also has a stables and carriage house designed by Newport native Dudley Newton (1845–1907).

Marble House

596 Bellevue Avenue
Newport, RI 02840
Phone: 401-847-2445
www.newportmansions.org

Of all of Newport's summer cottages, Marble House was the most costly to build. The construction expense was approximately $11 million (roughly equivalent to $270 million today). This is perhaps the most opulent of the houses in Newport.

The building of Marble House began in 1888 and was completed in 1892. This was built for William K. Vanderbilt (1849–1920), a grandson of "The Commodore" Cornelius Vanderbilt I (1794–1877), who established the family's fortune in steamships and railroads. William was one of a generation of Vanderbilt brothers who built several mansions that are open to the public today as museums: Cornelius II built The Breakers (1895) in Newport (see page 186), and Frederick built Newport's Rough Point (1892), which later became the home of Doris Duke (see page 183). Frederick also built a house at Hyde Park, New York, overlooking the Hudson River (1899). And it was the youngest of the brothers, George Washington, who had Biltmore (1895) constructed in Asheville, North Carolina. Of these, three are the work of Richard Morris Hunt (1827–1895): Marble House, The Breakers, and Biltmore.

William built Marble House as a gift for his wife Alva Vanderbilt (1853–1933) and presented it to her for her thirty-ninth birthday. The model was the Petit Trianon at Versailles. The house has about a half million cubic feet of marble from quarries in America, Europe, and Africa. There are fifty-two rooms covering 28,800 square feet.

When William and Alva divorced in 1895, she retained ownership of the house. She went on to marry Oliver H. P. Belmont, and they summered at Belcourt Castle just a short distance down Bellevue Avenue. In 1932 she sold the Marble House to Frederick H. Prince. The house and its contents were acquired by The Preservation Society of Newport County in 1963.

A tour of Marble House includes the first floor, second floor, and basement. The marble in the entrance hall, both floor and walls, is from Siena,

MARBLE HOUSE

*Gavin Ashworth photo courtesy
of The Preservation Society of
Newport County*

Italy. The tour progresses through the dining room, with its Numidian marble from North Africa, the library/morning room, the Gothic room, and the gold room, which served as a reception room and ballroom. Visitors continue up the grand staircase to the bedrooms, and then down the servants' stairs to the kitchen. Be sure to walk the back lawn to the Chinese Tea House (1914), which overlooks the Cliff Walk and the Atlantic Ocean.

Rosecliff

548 Bellevue Avenue
Newport, RI 02840
Phone: 401-847-5793
www.newportmansions.org

Rosecliff was the summer home of Mr. and Mrs. Hermann Oelrichs. Mr. Oelrichs (1850–1906) made his fortune in steamships. Mrs. Oelrich's maiden name was Theresa Fair (1869–1926). She was an heiress whose father was a developer of a mine at the Comstock Silver Lode in Nevada. They met at the Casino in Newport, were married in 1890, and lived in New York City. The following year they acquired this property as their summer home.

The wooden house they bought had been home to George Bancroft (1800–1891). Bancroft was from Worcester, Massachusetts, and had a distinguished career. As secretary of the Navy he established the United States Naval Academy at Annapolis in 1845. He was a statesman, a strong proponent of secondary education, the author of several history books, and a horticulturist. He cultivated the "American Beauty" rose. Because his rose gardens overlooked the Cliff Walk, the estate came to be known as Rosecliff.

In 1898 the Oelrichs had the wooden house demolished. They hired Stanford White (1853–1906) to design this home. White's model was the Grand Trianon at Versailles. Interestingly, the exterior here has a cap of glazed terra cotta. The project was completed in 1902 at a cost of $2.5 million. The house has 28,800 square feet, and there are thirty rooms.

Mr. Oelrichs died at sea in 1906; Mrs. Oelrichs died in 1926. Rosecliff was inherited by their son Hermann Jr. He continued to summer here. An occasional house guest was American songwriter and composer Cole Porter (1891–1964). He and Hermann would play table tennis in the ballroom, and it is believed that Porter composed some of his songs here.

Hermann sold the house for $21,000 in 1941. There was a series of owners. The last to own Rosecliff were Mrs. and Mrs. J. Edgar Monroe of New Orleans. In 1971 they donated the estate, the furnishings they had accumulated, and an endowment to The Preservation Society of Newport County.

A tour of the first floor starts in the salon and then proceeds to the ballroom, which is the largest in Newport, measuring forty feet by eighty feet. This room is often used for wedding receptions, corporate parties, and other special functions. Next are the billiard room, marble hall, and dining room. The tour continues upstairs by way of the heart-shaped grand staircase. It is made of Caen stone from France, is rococo in style, and is a copy of one in the eighteenth-century town hall in Nancy, France.

On the second floor there are several galleries in which special exhibits are mounted.

Several movies have been filmed in part at Rosecliff. These include *The Great Gatsby* (1973), starring Mia Farrow and Robert Redford; *True Lies* (1994), with Arnold Schwarzeneggar and Jamie Lee Curtis; *The Betsy* (1977), starring Sir Lawrence Olivier, Katherine Ross, and Robert Duval; *Amistad* (1997), with Morgan Freeman and Anthony Hopkins; and *27 Dresses* (2008), starring Katherine Heigl.

On leaving the house, be sure to visit the rose garden. This leads to the fountain and lawn at the back of the house, both of which overlook the Atlantic Ocean.

Samuel Whitehorne House

416 Thames Street
Newport, RI 02840
Phone: 401-847-2448
www.newportrestoration.org

Samuel Whitehorne (1779–1844) made his fortune in a variety of ways: in shipping, as the proprietor of an iron foundry, as a rum distiller, and as a banker. In 1843 two of his ships were lost at sea. As a consequence he went bankrupt. The house was then sold and over the years was divided into shops and apartments. The Newport Restoration Foundation bought the Whitehorne House in 1969 and restored it between 1970 and 1974.

The Whitehorne House is an imposing red-brick Federal-style building dating to 1811. It is a three-story house with a hipped roof, four corner chimneys, and a central cupola that was added around 1850. When built, the house faced bustling Newport Harbor, wharves, and tall ships.

The white classical portico on Thames Street frames the door, which leads to a great central hall. The house displays Doris Duke's outstanding collection of eighteenth-century Rhode Island furniture. There are pieces by the renowned Newport cabinetmakers the Townsends, the Goddards, Holmes Weaver, and Benjamin Baker. There is also a formal garden in back of the house, which visitors may see and enjoy.

Rough Point

680 Bellevue Avenue
Newport, RI 02840
Phone: 401-847-8344
www.newportmansions.org

Rough Point was one of several homes of Doris Duke (1912–1993), tobacco heiress, preservationist, philanthropist, art collector, horticulturist, and socialite. When her father James Buchanan Duke (1856–1925) died, twelve-year-old Doris inherited this and all his houses, as well as his vast fortune. In 1968 Miss Duke founded the Newport Restoration Foundation, which after her death opened this property to the public for tours.

This English Tudor/Elizabethan Revival mansion dates to 1887–1891. It was built for Frederick W. Vanderbilt, whose brothers Cornelius II (see page 186) and William K. (see page 177) also built summer homes in Newport. Frederick later built another home in Hyde Park, New York. The house is built of rough-hewn gray-brown granite. It was designed by the architectural firm of Peabody and Stearns. In 1906 Rough Point was sold to the Leeds family, who in turn sold it to Mr. Duke in 1922. Horace Trumbauer (1868–1938) was hired to make several alterations to the house, including the addition of two wings and a solarium looking out onto the Atlantic Ocean. On the property there are topiary figures that recall two of Miss Duke's pets: camels Princess and Baby.

The original landscaping was the 1890 work of Frederick Law Olmsted (see page 64). It includes a geometric formal garden, an arboretum, and a rose garden. More than thirty-five varieties of dahlias are planted here, as well as a kitchen garden with vegetables and herbs.

THE GREAT HALL IN
THE BREAKERS

*Gavin Ashworth photo courtesy
of The Preservation Society of
Newport County*

The Breakers

44 Ochre Point Avenue
Newport, RI 02840
Phone: 401-847-1000
www.newportmansions.org

The Breakers was built in 1895 as a summer home for Cornelius Vanderbilt II (1843–1899). His grandfather Cornelius Vanderbilt I (1794–1877) (known as "The Commodore") began the family's business in transportation—first steamships and then railroads. By 1885 there was more money in the Vanderbilt family fortune then there was in the United States Treasury.

Cornelius Vanderbilt II and his family lived in New York City in a 156-room mansion at the corner of Fifth Avenue and Fifty-Seventh Street (the site of the Bergdorf Goodman department store today). In 1885 he bought The Breakers property from Pierre Lorillard IV to be his summer estate. On this site there was a large wooden Queen Anne–style house. It burned down in 1892, and this house was built on its site. The architect was Richard Morris Hunt (1827–1895), the "Dean of American Architecture." Hunt also designed other Vanderbilt houses: Biltmore in Asheville, North Carolina, and Marble House in Newport.

Mrs. & Mrs. Vanderbilt had seven children. The youngest was Gladys (1886–1965), who married the Hungarian Count Laszlo Szechenyi (1879–1938). When her mother died in 1936, Gladys inherited the house. She leased the first floor of The Breakers (at a cost of one dollar a year) to The Preservation Society of Newport County soon after it was founded in 1945. Admission was charged (fifty cents per person) and tours were given. The money raised here funded the restoration of the eighteenth-century Hunter House (see page 169), which in turn was also opened to the public for tours. After her death in 1965, Gladys's heirs sold The Breakers to the Society for a nominal fee.

Another of the Vanderbilts' seven children was Reginald Claypoole Vanderbilt (1880–1925). His daughter is Gloria Vanderbilt (b. 1924). Gloria is the mother of television personality, news anchor, and author Anderson Cooper (b. 1967).

During the Gilded Age following the Civil War, Newport became

America's most fashionable resort. Millionaires from New York City and elsewhere chose to summer here and to compete with each other in the building of large and opulent summer "cottages." Not to be outdone, Cornelius Vanderbilt II built the most massive of Newport's summer cottages, The Breakers.

The Breakers boasts seventy rooms covering 138,300 square feet. Richard Morris Hunt designed this Italian Renaissance palace around the Great Hall, which is approximately fifty feet in height, length, and width. Built as a place for entertainment and large, lavish parties, The Breakers had a staff of forty servants.

From the Great Hall, visitors progress to other rooms in various styles: the breakfast room with its Louis XV–style wall panels imported from France, then on to the Italian Renaissance dining room, the billiard room, the morning room, the library, the eighteenth-century French–style bedrooms, and the loggia/porch overlooking the Cliff Walk and the Atlantic Ocean. The tour ends with a visit to the servants' wing with its cavernous kitchen and pantry. Outside the house visitors are free to explore the thirteen-acre property and, in season, the Children's Play Cottage and the Stables, with its extensive collection of carriages and sleighs.

There are two tours at The Breakers. The first tour guides visitors through the sumptuous first and second floors and ends in the kitchen and pantry. The second is the "Beneath The Breakers" tour, which explores a portion of the property that until recently was hidden from public view. The Beneath The Breakers tour begins in the Superintendent's Cottage and continues downstairs to the boiler room. Visitors are then led down the three hundred fifty foot underground tunnel to the basement of this great house to see its original plumbing and electrical fixtures, wine cellar, and other work areas.

The Elms

367 Bellevue Avenue
Newport, RI 02840
Phone: 401-847-0478
www.newportmansions.org

The Elms was built in 1901 as a summer house for Edward Julius Berwind (1848–1936). Mr. Berwind was originally from Philadelphia. He was an extremely successful coal magnate and was based in New York City. In 1888 he and Mrs. Berwind (née Sarah Vesta Herminie Torrey, 1856–1922) bought this property and its wooden Italianate house. Eleven years later they had that house demolished and replaced it with this mansion.

The architect Berwind commissioned was Horace Trumbauer (1868–1938). Like Mr. Berwind, Trumbauer was from Philadelphia. Some of his best known works are the chapel and other buildings at Duke University, the Philadelphia Art Museum, and Harvard University's Widener Library. Here Trumbauer's inspiration was the eighteenth-century Chateau d'Asnières, which stands near Paris. When completed in 1901, this was the first fully electrified house in Newport and had no gas backup. The cost of building The Elms was $1.4 million. There are forty-eight rooms, and the size of the house is 60,000 square feet.

The Berwinds never had any children. Mrs. Berwind predeceased her husband. His sister Miss Julia Berwind (1865–1961) became his hostess and heir. She continued to summer here. On her death on 1961, the property passed to a nephew who had the furniture, artwork, and collections of The Elms sold at auction. The house was to go to a developer and be demolished. Instead, The Preservation Society of Newport County was able to buy the house through the generosity of donors. Every effort is being made to retrieve what was sold at the auction (this is an ongoing effort). Where original pieces have not been brought back, similar works are now in place. Progressing from room to room, there are on display a series of room portraits that date to the early 1950s. The rooms look very much as they did when the family was in residence.

The Berwinds were passionate art collectors. With the advice and expertise of the Parisian designer Jules Allard (1832–1907), they gathered a sizable collection of eighteenth-century French art, Venetian art, Asian art, and other antiques.

One of the highlights of the house tour is the light-filled conservatory, which was inspired by eighteenth-century French orangeries. The dining room is eighteenth-century Venetian in style, its walls hung with a series of paintings from a palace in Venice. Some of the paintings in this collection are massive, and all date to the early eighteenth century. By contrast, the breakfast room is fitted with eighteenth-century Chinese lacquer panels.

At the back of the house, one can find a terrace, an expansive lawn, and an immense cluster of weeping beech trees. Beyond that there are two pavilion tea houses, the stables and carriage house, the garden alley, fountains, and a sunken garden.

The Elms offers two tours. The first is a walk through the family's area of the house with its exquisite decor. The other is the Servant Life Tour, on which visitors see the parts of the house where the staff lived and worked: the basement with its laundry room, kitchens, and pantries; the sub-basement with its furnaces and coal tunnel; the third-floor staff living quarters; and a panoramic view of Newport from the roof.

THE ELMS

Gavin Ashworth photo courtesy of The Preservation Society of Newport County

The Brayton House at Green Animals

Green Animals Topiary Garden

380 Cory's Lane

Portsmouth, RI 02871

Phone: 401-683-1267

www.newportmansions.org

Green Animals Topiary Garden sits on seven emerald acres overlooking placid Narragansett Bay. In 1860, Providence mill owner Amasa Manton built the white clapboard house as a summer home for his family. Nearby were the kitchen (a separate building), icehouse, greenhouse, barn, gardener's cottage, fruit trees, vegetable gardens, flower gardens, and pasture. In 1872 the property was sold to Thomas Brayton (1844–1939), the treasurer and part-owner of a cotton mill in Fall River, Massachusetts. Mr. and Mrs. Brayton and their four children lived in Fall River and would summer here. In summer Mr. Brayton commuted to work in Fall River by railroad. The tracks run parallel to the edge of the bay, and Mr. Brayton had his own small depot at the foot of his property.

When Mr. Brayton died in 1939, the property went to two of his children: Alice and Edward. Edward sold his share to Alice for one dollar, and she lived here year round beginning in 1940, naming the property Green Animals. Miss Alice Brayton (1878–1972) was a horticulturist, historian, and writer. She also devoted much of her time to charitable causes. Miss Brayton was active in Newport society. In 1947 she hosted a coming-out party for debutante Jacqueline Bouvier here, and some years later President and Mrs. Kennedy visited Green Animals with their children Caroline and John John. Alice never married, and when she died at the age of ninety-four in 1972, she bequeathed her beloved estate to The Preservation Society of Newport County.

The size of the house is 10,500 square feet. A visit features the sitting room, family dining room, library, parlor, and servant dining room on the first floor. The house has European and American furniture, paintings, and decorative arts. On the second floor, two bedrooms are furnished with original pieces. A special treat is an antique toy museum on the second floor, which includes doll houses, dolls, toy soldiers, and stuffed animals.

In 1905, Alice's father hired Jose Carreiro to be the property superintendent. Mr. Carriero was from Portugal, and he remembered the topiaries he had seen there as a boy. He began to cultivate similar topiaries on the property. When he retired in 1945 his son-in-law George Mendonca became superintendent. George retired in 1985, and today the staff of the Newport Mansions maintains the gardens. The green animals have multiplied over the years, and the garden is populated with a menagerie of creatures: an elephant, a giraffe, a lion, bears (both large and small), dogs, birds, and a multitude of other animals. These were created from California privet, yew, and English or Japanese boxwood. There is also a fishpond, a pet cemetery, flower beds, arbors, reed grasses, a bamboo grove, fruit trees, and a vegetable garden (the produce is given to charity).

No visit to Green Animals is complete without a few moments sitting in a rocker on the house's front porch overlooking tranquil Narragansett Bay.

John Brown House Museum

52 Power Street

Providence, RI 02906

Phone: 401-273-7507

www.rihs.org

"... the most magnificent and elegant private house I have ever seen on this continent."

—JOHN QUINCY ADAMS

John Brown (1736–1803) was a Patriot and a politician. He was also a merchant and a slave trader. By contrast, his brother Moses was an abolitionist, and their debate on the subject of slavery was a very public one. Another brother, Joseph, was an amateur architect and designed this house for his brother in 1786. It was completed two years later. Together with another brother, Nicholas, the Browns founded Brown University.

While George Washington did not sleep here, he was a guest for tea. Abigail Adams was also a guest here, as was her son John Quincy Adams.

In 1901 the house was sold to Marsden J. Perry, who made some changes. It was later sold to John Nicholas Brown in 1936, who in turn donated it to the Rhode Island Historical Society so that it could be opened to the public as a museum.

This is a three-story brick mansion with four chimneys and a hip roof surrounded by a balustrade. In front of the front door there is a sandstone portico supported by Doric columns. And over the portico there is a Palladian window. Andrea Palladio (1508–1580) was an Italian Renaissance architect known in part for his use of one central round-topped window flanked by two smaller windows. The grand hall is flanked by two large rooms on either side. The period pieces housed here include furnishings original to the Brown family.

The house is sited on a hill, and in the back the extensive property slopes down to Benefit Street. It is planted with tall trees and is the setting for outdoor concerts in summer.

Pendleton House

Museum of the Rhode Island School of Design

224 Benefit Street

Providence, RI 02903

Phone: 401-454-6500

http://risdmuseum.org

Pendleton House is a part of the Museum of the Rhode Island School of Design. It is a replica of a 1799 Federal-style house at 72 Waterman Street in Providence. That was the home of Charles L. Pendleton (1846–1904), who gave his extensive collection of American and European furniture, paintings, silver, and other decorative arts to the Rhode Island School of Design with the understanding that the collection would be displayed in an appropriate building.

The collection was acquired in 1904. Two years later the Pendleton House we see today was designed by the architectural firm of Stone, Carpenter, and Willson. It was the first museum wing anywhere devoted solely to American decorative arts. The first floor by and large replicates Pendleton's home. The collection has exceptionally fine examples of eighteenth-century furniture from Newport, Boston, New York, and Philadelphia. The Newport collection includes six pieces of furniture made by the renowned cabinetmakers the Goddards and the Townsends. On the second floor of the house there are more American period rooms.

Pendleton House is contiguous with the rest of the RISD Museum, which arguably has the finest and most diverse art collection in America for a museum its size: art which is Ancient, Asian, European (medieval to contemporary), and American (colonial to the present). To name a few of the artists whose art is in the permanent collection, there are works by Tiepolo, Reynolds, Rodin, Monet, Picasso, Nevelson, Warhol, and RISD alumnus Chihuly.

VERMONT

Old Stone House Museum

Old Stone House Road
Brownington, VT 05860
Phone: 802-754-2022
http://oldstonehousemuseum.org

The Old Stone House is one of several historic buildings in the Brownington Historic District of Vermont's Northeast Kingdom. The house is also known as Athenian Hall. It was the work and dream of Alexander Twilight (1795–1857). A Vermont native, Twighlight is believed to be the first African American to receive a college degree from an American school (Vermont's Middlebury College, in 1823). After graduation he wore many hats as a Congregationalist minister, politician, and principal of the Orleans County Grammar School. Students whose homes were a distance from the school often boarded with Mr. and Mrs. Twighlight and other families in the village. From 1834 to 1836, Athenian Hall was built to be a student dormitory for boys and girls. A four-story granite building, it ceased to be a dormitory in 1856, was empty for many years, and was bought at auction in 1918 by the Orleans Historical Society for five hundred dollars. The Society opened the house as a museum in 1925. The Brownington Historic District was placed on the US National Register of Historic Places in 1973.

Other sites open to the public within the village include Alexander Twighlight's house (1830), Cyrus Eaton House (1834), Samuel Read Hall House (1831), Brownington Congregational Church and cemetery, Prospect Hill and Observatory Tower, a blacksmith shop, barns, the grammar school, and a perennial garden.

Rokeby Museum Main House

4334 Route 7
Ferrisburgh, VT 05456
Phone: 802-877-3406
http://rokeby.org

The Rokeby Museum is a ninety-acre historic farm near the shores of Lake Champlain. It was originally the Dakin family farm. In the 1780s they built a modest house. Then Thomas Robinson, a Quaker from Newport, Rhode Island, bought the Dakin farm in 1793. He added the two-story wooden nucleus of the house in the then popular Federal style in 1814. This was home to four generations of the Robinson family. The Robinsons were farmers, millers, authors, and artists. They were also abolitionists, and this was a stop on the Underground Railroad in the 1830s and 1840s. The Main House is furnished with Robinson family furniture, artwork, books, china, and other possessions acquired over two hundred years.

Be sure to tour the property. The farm's other sites include the smoke house, hen house, creamery, tool shed and slaughterhouse, and the granary. The Underground Railroad Education Center has an exhibit: *Free and Safe: The Underground Railroad in Vermont.*

Hildene

1005 Hildene Road
Manchester, VT 05254
Phone: 802-362-1788
www.hildene.org

The name "Hildene" has its roots in the Old English word for a pastoral setting that includes a stream, a hill, and a valley. An overlook above the Battenkill Valley provided a picturesque and idyllic site for the summer home of Robert Todd Lincoln (1843–1926), son of Abraham Lincoln.

Robert first visited this area with his mother and brother Tad in 1864. Robert had just graduated from Harvard College and turned twenty-one that summer. Wishing to escape Washington's summer heat and humidity, they sojourned at Equinox House in Manchester.

Of President Lincoln's four children, Robert was the only one to live to adulthood. He had a distinguished career as an attorney, statesman, and businessman, serving as the secretary of war under two presidents and later as president of the Pullman Palace Car Company.

The Boston architectural firm Shepley, Rutan, and Coolidge designed this Georgian Revival home. It took two years to build, and Robert and his wife Mary Harlan Lincoln and their children first enjoyed their new summer house in 1905. Three years later, Robert gifted Mary an Aeolian pipe organ, complete with more than nine hundred pipes. The organ has been restored and is played daily to the delight of visitors. There is Lincoln furniture throughout the house, as well as other objects that belonged to Robert and his parents. The house is 8,000 square feet, and it has twenty-four rooms, a basement, and an attic. The cost of construction was approximately sixty-three thousand dollars.

Beyond the house, be sure to explore the 412-acre estate, which is split between a bluff above and meadows below. There is a formal garden, the cutting and kitchen gardens, twelve miles of walking trails, and fields. The barn has been transformed into the welcome center and museum store. There are interactive displays, introductory films, a telegraph, an observation beehive, and a model Pullman train circling the perimeter at ceiling level. Visitors will see the Sunbeam, a restored Pullman Palace train car. The exhibit *Many Voices* focuses on those who were associated

HILDENE

Courtesy of Hildene

with the Pullman Company: a wealthy passenger, black porters, and others. A more recent addition to the property, the Hildene Farm Goat Dairy is a cheese-making facility powered by renewable energy. It houses a milking herd of Nubian goats.

Abraham and Mary Todd Lincoln have no living descendants today. Robert's granddaughter Mary Lincoln Beckwith lived here. She died in 1975, and three years later the Friends of Hildene, a nonprofit organization, bought the estate, opened it to the public, and have since restored its buildings and gardens. In recent years, the resources and assets of the entire estate have been put to use, not only for touring guests, but also as a place for educational programming at many levels. Hildene's future is its mission: "Values into Action."

Calvin Coolidge Homestead

3780 Route 100A

Plymouth, VT 05056

Phone: 802-672-3773

www.nps.gov/nr/travel/presidents/calvin_coolidge_homestead

"I love Vermont because of her hills and valleys, her scenery and invigorating climate, but most of all because of her indomitable people."

—CALVIN COOLIDGE

The Plymouth Historic District has many sites associated with America's thirtieth president, John Calvin Coolidge (1872–1933). He was born in a small house attached to his father's general store on July 4, 1872. Four years later the family moved across the street to this modest one-and-a-half-story wood-frame clapboard house. They later added a front porch, bay windows, and other improvements. "Cal," as he was known to his family, lived much of his life in Massachusetts, where he became governor and then later vice president under President Warren G. Harding (1865–1923). Vice President Coolidge was here when President Harding died, and he took the oath of office by the light of a kerosene lamp in the sitting room. His father, a justice of the peace, administered the oath.

President Coolidge won the presidential election in 1924 and served one full term. He left office in 1929 and died four years later. Coolidge is buried in Plymouth Notch Cemetery in his family's plot. The house was inherited by his son John, who, in 1956, donated it and its contents to the state of Vermont.

A walk through the village will lead visitors to many sites the President knew: the Post Office, the old Coolidge house and general store, the one-room schoolhouse, several houses, Plymouth Notch Cemetery, and Union Christian Church.

CALVIN COOLIDGE
HOMESTEAD,
PLYMOUTH, VERMONT

Photograph by Alois Mayer,

© Vermont Photographics

The Dwellings of Shelburne Museum

6000 Shelburne Road

Shelburne, VT 05482

Phone: 802-985-3346

http://shelburnemuseum.org

The Shelburne Museum is a village of buildings clustered near the shores of Lake Champlain and not far from Burlington. The museum was founded in 1947 by Electra Havemeyer Webb (1888–1960). Mrs. Webb and her husband James Watson Webb (1884–1960), a Vanderbilt descendant, were based in New York City. She had inherited her parents' collection of art: paintings by Old Masters, French impressionist artists, and bronzes, both European and American. Electra, however, turned her attention to collecting works in a genre that was little recognized or appreciated at that time: American folk art. She would summer in this area and began Shelburne Museum to house and display her collections. Today the museum has more than 150,000 objects housed in thirty-eight buildings, twenty-five of which have been moved to this forty-five-acre site. These include house museums. In addition to the houses, readers are encouraged to visit other sites at the museum: a lighthouse, meeting house, steamboat, general store, covered bridge, circus building, blacksmith shop, apothecary shop, round barn, schoolhouse, galleries in the Pizzagalli Center, and other buildings.

Electra Havemeyer Webb New York City Apartment

The Electra Havemeyer Webb Memorial Building was commissioned by her children in 1960. It is a Greek Revival design modeled after the 1843 Wilcox-Curtis House in Orwell, Vermont. It includes six rooms from the Webbs' New York City apartment at 740 Park Avenue. Their art collection is displayed here as it was in their apartment. The paintings include works by Rembrandt van Rijn and impressionist artists Claude Monet, Édouard Manet, and Edgar Degas. The American impressionist artist Mary Cassatt is also represented. Cassatt was a friend of Mrs. Webb's parents. She painted a portrait of Electra and her mother which hangs here. The walls, the art, and the furniture re-create the apartment Mrs. Webb knew.

Jail

And now for historic housing which none would aspire to live in. This is the old jail from Castleton, Vermont, built in 1890. Having fallen into disuse, it was sold to the Shelburne Museum in 1953. The jail weighs fifty tons, and it was sold for one dollar per ton. The sixty-four-mile journey from Castleton to Shelburne took three days.

The jail is constructed from slate mined in the western part of Vermont in an area bordering New York State. The door is iron, and within the jail there are two cells, an office for the jailkeeper, and very little daylight.

Prentis House

Saltbox houses, like this one, were very common in early New England, and their name derives from the fact that their outer forms so closely resembled the saltboxes used in kitchens at the time. If a lean-to were added to a house, the saltbox appearance was created. More often than not, add-ons were made as a family grew in number.

The Prentis House dates to 1773. It was built for the Dickensen family in Hadley, Massachusetts, and moved to this site in 1953. The large central chimney has seven flues on the first floor and rises to a beehive on the second. The house displays seventeenth- and eighteenth-century decorative arts: furniture, textiles, English delftware, and other items.

Settlers' House and Barn

Settlers' House is, essentially, a log cabin. Built in 1845, it is very typical of the type of temporary housing built for settlers, trappers, and loggers in the late-eighteenth to early-nineteenth century. This house was built for French Canadian lumberjacks and was moved the Shelburne Museum in 1955.

The timber used here is hand-hewn pine and beech. The house has two rooms and an open-hearth fireplace. There is a vegetable garden and a clay-bake oven where interpreters demonstrate early cooking methods and other skills.

Stencil House

Stencil House is very suitably named. Its plain, weathered clapboard exterior belies what awaits inside.

The house was built in Columbus, New York, in 1804. The interior floor plan is typical and predictable: a large central chimney surrounded by four rooms on the first floor. What is atypical, however, is the extensive and rare stencil work. When the house was acquired by Shelburne Museum in 1953, and when it was ready to be moved to this site, it was discovered that some of the old wallpapers (several layers of them) were cracking and peeling. Removing the papers revealed stenciling beneath. Not just border stenciling, but entire walls covered with the stenciler's art, and not on plaster, but on the wall boards. There is evidence of this in the entrance hallway, the dining room, and the parlor. To complete the experience, Stencil House has been furnished with eighteenth-century furniture and decorative items.

Marsh-Billings-Rockefeller National Historic Park

54 Elm Street
Woodstock, VT 05091
Phone: 802-457-3368, x 222
www.nps.gov/mabi

"... America's leading conservationist."

—LADY BIRD JOHNSON, SPEAKING OF
LAURANCE S. ROCKEFELLER

This property's tale begins in 1805. Charles Marsh (1755–1849), a successful attorney, built this house in the Federal style. His son George Perkins Marsh (1801–1882) followed his father's footsteps into law. The younger Marsh was also an early conservationist and in 1864 wrote *Man and Nature, or the Physical Geography as Modified by Human Behavior.*

In 1869 the estate was bought by Frederick H. Billings (1823–1890), who, as it happens, was also a lawyer and conservationist. Billings earned his living as an attorney during the California Gold Rush. He was also a founder and president of the Northern Pacific Railroad. Between 1869 and 1881, Billings made a number of changes to this house, transforming it from a Federal- to a Queen Anne–style mansion. This was the work of architect Henry Hudson Holly (1834–1892). And across the road, Billings established a farm. His daughter Mary Billings French (1910–1997) married Laurance S. Rockefeller (1910–2004) in 1934. The Rockefeller family funded the opening or improvement of more than twenty national parks. In like spirit, Laurance was a conservationist and an advisor to a number of US presidents. President George H. W. Bush awarded Rockefeller the Congressional Gold Medal in 1991 in recognition of his work and contributions. Laurance and Mary donated the house and property to the American people in 1992.

A visit to the park starts at the 1895 Carriage Barn and visitor center. Tours are given of the mansion, which is an outstanding example of Queen Anne–style architecture. It houses an impressive collection of paintings by nineteenth-century American landscape artists Albert Bierstadt, Thomas Cole, Asher Durand, John Frederick Kensett, and others. Visitors are also welcome to visit the Billings Farm just steps away across the road. This is a working farm, and a visit includes the farmhouse. Beyond the farm and the mansion, the park has twenty miles of walking trails and carriage roads.

MARSH-BILLINGS-
ROCKEFELLER
MANSION

E. Sharron photo courtesy of
Marsh-Billings-Rockefeller NHP

Index